Six Under
After Five

Growing Old is Mandatory;
Growing Up is Optional

MEMOIRS
OF
LOWELL
LEFFLER

 FriesenPress

Suite 300 - 990 Fort St
Victoria, BC, V8V 3K2
Canada

www.friesenpress.com

ISBN
978-1-03-910823-3 (Hardcover)
978-1-03-910822-6 (Paperback)
978-1-03-910824-0 (eBook)

1. Biography & Autobiography, Personal Memoirs

Distributed to the trade by The Ingram Book Company

This book is dedicated to Olivia, Sloane, Brody, Cohen, Maeve, Chloe, Greta, and Briar. They truly are the "Eight Wonders" of our world of grandparenting.

As well, I need to thank "The Enemy." The reason grandchildren and grandparents get along so well is because they share a common enemy: "The Parents."

Andrea & Colin Hennel
Dustin & Sarah Leffler
Courtney & Matthew Hall

Table of Contents

Introduction

In the Beginning

The year 2020 will be forever remembered, in infamy, as the year of the COVID-19 pandemic. The Coronavirus started in Wuhan, China, in November of 2019 and by March, 2020, had spread its way across the globe. As we are now past its first anniversary, the ramifications to the world-wide economy and people everywhere are still being felt. Just when we began to think we had it under control, along comes winter, and the second wave hit. Once again, in an attempt to "flatten the curve," we were prevented from visiting loved ones and friends.

The one good thing that came out of the pandemic was that it gave me the time, in isolation, to write my book. I first began to contemplate writing an autobiography when I retired from education ten years earlier. However, during this time, we became *snowbirds* and began spending our winters in Arizona. There always seemed to be something more pressing to do than working on my book. Whether it was golf, pickleball, social hours, or quadding, life just kept getting in the way of my literary prowess.

In March, when we were all faced with quarantining ourselves inside our houses for several months, I searched for ways to prevent boredom. It all began with submitting a few Facebook stories for my "friends" to read. A snowbird friend, Vicki Syvertsen, from Minnesota, suggested I should write a daily blog outlining either current or past experiences, and post these on Facebook, each morning. And so, it began. I would wake up at 4:30 am each morning and jot down my thoughts. It's a sad commentary on life when you wait until you retire so you can sleep in and then find out you can't.

Each story's content was drawn from ideas and events that actually happened to me. While the truth was occasionally embellished, the result is more a snapshot of history than fiction. I attempted to present these ideas with the intent to make people laugh, as well as create the content I could use in my book.

I received so much positive feedback daily that I decided to go full steam ahead and work towards completing my autobiography. The purpose of this book is to provide my children, grandchildren, and anybody else who might be interested with insights about events that led me to become the person I am today. In no way do I condone many of the things I did when I was growing up. I would never have allowed our children to be so reckless, but those were different times. We lived by the adage, "If it didn't kill you, it made you stronger." Fortunately for me, I only got stronger, which was likely more luck than skill. To my grandchildren and great-grandchildren, as they say on television, please don't try any of these things at home.

The Name Game

The most challenging thing I encountered during all my writing was deciding on a book title. It took months of throwing away different ideas before I was finally able to settle on the one that I knew was "it." Since education had always been an integral part of my life, I was leaning towards something related to that. While the book contains many articles about education, the real focus was the life lessons I learned growing up.

It was a comment from a former colleague and friend, Barry Litun, that solidified my decision. As soon as I heard it, I knew this had to be the name of the book. Let me explain.

When I retired from the Prairie Rose School Division back in 2010, I had several retirement functions. I guess everyone was thrilled I was finally leaving. One of the celebrations was held in Edmonton and sponsored by CASS, the College of Alberta School Superintendents. There were many of my Superintendent colleagues in attendance. When I was introduced and asked to say a few words, apparently, I said one thing of significance. Years later, colleagues have reminded me they never forgot what I told them.

I finished off my short talk with a joke. I explained that I was already planning for the future. I wanted to take care of all my funeral arrangements so my family would not be burdened with them. Furthermore, I was retiring in Bow Island, Alberta, where I had already agreed to take over management of the golf course. The golf course shares a common perimeter with the cemetery.

I explained that since I was going to be management, I could do something no one else could do. I described that I had purchased a small plot of land where I was to be buried. It was located between hole #5 putting green and the tee-off box for hole #6. By being buried in that location, I would finally accomplish something I could never do when I was alive. That was to be "Six Under After Five."

When I received an email from Barry who I mentioned above, he reminded me of the joke I had told ten years earlier. It struck me like a bolt of lightning that there could only be one name for my book; Six Under After Five. This name relates to my passion for golf and the fact I must face my own mortality, and the only way to do that is to go out laughing.

The Early Years

A Needle in a Haystack

My paternal Grandfather, Edward Leffler, was born in Lipniaka, Russia, on August 17, 1885. In 1905, it looked like war was breaking out, and Edward feared he would be conscripted into the Russian Army. He saved up enough money to pay a stranger who could help smuggle him out of Russia.

Along with several friends, they were instructed to meet a man in an isolated area, close to a swift-flowing river. This man had to carry each person on his back across the stream. He was the only one who knew the way across safely. As soon as they reached the opposite shore, they ran to a nearby barn and hid under the hay. They were given firm directions not to move under any circumstances. When the Russian soldiers searched for runaways, they would use pitchforks to stab into the hay. Deserters who were found hiding were immediately executed.

The next day, they were led away and eventually reached safety in Europe. He purchased a ticket on a ship bound for the United States. He landed in Seattle and rode a boxcar to Winnipeg, Manitoba. Here he got a job working for the Canadian National Railway. He worked there until he purchased some farmland in Runnymede, Saskatchewan. During his time in Winnipeg, he met and married Clara Domke.

My Grandmother, Clara Domke, was born in Puriellis, Russia, on June 15, 1891. When she was 21, she left everything behind and emigrated by herself. She came to Canada by ship. When they were a few days out of landing in Nova Scotia, they heard distress signals coming from another vessel that you may have heard of. Its name was the Titanic. Fortunately for us, she was on the ship that didn't sink.

In 1919, for $160, Edward and Clara purchased some land near Runnymede, Saskatchewan. Here, they built a home and a barn and cleared the land. Several years later, they lost the farm due to the depression.

In 1927, they again purchased some land not far from the first farm they lost. Their land was situated beside the local school called "Memorial." My Grandparents became the school's caretakers, and they also ended up boarding the teacher. My Grandfather was very civic-minded and, as a result, became the Chairman of the local School Board.

In 1952, he hired a rookie teacher named Sabina Nawolski. She was fresh out of Normal School in Saskatoon. Normal School was a college established for the purpose of training new teachers. The teachers only spent a couple of months training before they were ready to teach. These inexperienced teachers often ended up with assignments that included multiple grades in one-room school-houses across the province. Sabina had grown up in Cody, so she was very familiar with this area and excited about returning home to teach. Who is this Sabina, you may ask?

Since my dad was still living at home and the two of them were living under the same roof, it was inevitable they would get together. They were married on April 18, 1953. My mother was four years older than my dad, so he was only 19 years old when they got married. It was a little joke in our family that my mother had robbed the cradle. Interestingly enough, when I married Irene, I was only 20 years old, while she was 24. I often wondered if this was genetic until my son ended up marrying a younger woman and breaking the mold.

I am confident some of you will do the math and discover I was born less than five months after being married. I don't remember them ever telling me I was a preemie, and I am pretty sure there has only been one virgin birth in 2000 years of prior history. I guess living under the same roof, with no television and not much else to do, it was inevitable that passions might run high.

Lost at Birth

The following could only happen in Saskatchewan. Before I arrived in the world, my parents lived on a farm close to the little town of Runnymede, just a few miles from the Manitoba border. While it may share its namesake, this is NOT the place in England where they signed the Magna Carta in 1215 AD. The closest hospital was about an hour away, in the city of Yorkton. Therefore, when the famous day of September 6, 1953, arrived, I was delivered, kicking and screaming at the Yorkton Hospital. I was born very young for my age.

I don't remember my mother describing my birth as particularly difficult. After all, women have built-in higher pain tolerance for the sole purpose of childbirth. This feature has evolved over the years to make the process of delivery relatively painless. Women are so lucky; they get all the breaks in life. If reincarnation exists, and I am worthy, maybe I will be allowed to come back as a woman and feel what it is like to have the final say in everything. If my wife reads this, you will know who killed me.

To have a birth certificate issued, the hospital was responsible for sending the government all the names of babies born each day. Somehow my records were lost, misplaced, or stolen. When they were finally found six days after my birth, the paperwork sent in for me indicted I was not born until September 12. Either this was the most grueling labour in history, or my mother had too much pain killer during the ordeal and was hallucinating. In any event, we always celebrated my birthday on September 6, so that was the day I eagerly anticipated.

It wouldn't seem that having an incorrect birthdate would be such a big deal, but all through my life, it was the "Bane of My Existence." You probably think I should feel fortunate to get to celebrate two birthdays every year. Think of "those poor folk" born on February 29 during a leap year. They only get to celebrate their birthday every four years. I can't wait to turn 136 this year by celebrating two birthdays.

The first time this "Dual Birthday Curse" struck was when I reached the ripe old age of 16. The day was rapidly approaching when I would enter this first phase of adulthood. Not quite "Freedom 55," but still independence. The Holy Grail of any male teenager is the day they receive their coveted driver's license.

We lived in Bow Island at the time. Since it was a small town, there was no licensing agency. The only option we had was having a testing instructor come out from Medicine Hat once a week. Because I had always celebrated my birthday on September 6, it never occurred to me I would not be "legal" until the 12th.

There was NO way I could wait six more, long days to get my license. Even though Mom explained I had no choice but to wait, I still decided to go in to check with the "Tester" and explain my predicament. He informed me there was nothing he could legally do about the situation. Even when I threatened to bring my mom down there to straighten him out, he still wouldn't relent.

However, he did gave me an option that somewhat helped ease my misery. He told me I could take the test's driving portion before turning 16. If I passed, I would still have to wait until the following week for it to become official. At least when I showed up the next week, I did not have to worry about failing. It would be nothing more than a rubber-stamping, and I would be a legal driver. To show my maturity, I immediately stopped my temper tantrum and told him I was good with that.

When the test day came, I had Mom ride with me in our half-ton truck downtown to the Community Center. This was where the examiner worked every Thursday. Together, we walked around the vehicle to ensure the lights and other equipment were working. Finally, the test began. Bow Island is not that big, and when he told me to drive south, I wondered if we would be going by our house. I was thinking that I hope Snoopy, our beagle, is not outside because he loves nothing more than going for rides in the truck.

As luck would have it, we did indeed drive by the house. When I looked in the rear-view mirror, guess what I saw. It was Snoopy running behind the truck, trying to catch us. I told the examiner I would stop and instruct Snoopy to go home. When I got out and yelled, Snoopy turned around and started slowly walking back to the house. As soon as I got back in the truck, he had already turned around and began chasing us again. When I got to the stop sign, he caught up to us and was barking at my door to get in.

I knew you were not allowed to have any pets with you during the test, so I was getting ready to drive off. The examiner told me he didn't want to run over the dog and we could let him in the truck. There we were, driving around, with Snoopy sitting almost on top of the evaluator, begging him to put his window down so he could put his head out and feel the rush of the wind.

We finished the test, and the last thing to do was wait while the instructor added up all the checkmarks. I was praying I had done well enough, so I didn't have to retake the test. He looked up and smiled and said, "I have some good news and some bad news." I had passed the test, but I still had to wait another week before he would stamp my license. That was the longest week of my life.

Of course, this life-altering error would haunt me further in the future. When I turned 18, I couldn't go to the bar for, you guessed it, six days. When I turned 55, I had to again wait for another %$#@& six days to retire. And of course, when I turned 65, I had to wait six days before I could claim my Old Age Security cheque.

I hope when my end comes, I will somehow be resurrected and hang around for another six days. I figure the only way to get back at the government bureaucracy that caused all my grief is to have my tombstone engraved with the following words. Lowell was born September 6, just like Panasonic, ahead of his time.

Breaking Bad

When we first moved to Grassy Lake, Alberta, our family of five lived in a one-bedroom teacherage. My sisters, Wendy and Ruby, and I slept on a pull-out couch in the living room. The house was located just off the school grounds, about 100 yards from the school. Before I was old enough to attend school, I enjoyed playing with the "older" kids during recess and lunch hours. One of my favourite things to do was the high jump. It involved jumping over a bar into a pit of sand. The sand was supposed to help soften your landing if you didn't land on your feet. In those days, the only jumping style used was the "scissors" because landing on any part of your body, other than your feet, hurt too much.

I was always short for my age. It seemed like I had to try extra hard to clear the bar compared to my taller friends. On one fateful day, I was leaping particularly well and was closing in on my record personal best. I remember psyching up and convincing myself I could fly if I ran fast enough. I took off towards the bar like I was being chased by hungry demons. As I planted my foot and began my lift-off, I felt my foot slide forward, and I became airborne but out of control.

Rather than having my feet absorb the impact of gravity, my left arm supplied the cushioning. I heard a snap and felt the pain shoot up my arm. When I looked down, my hand was hanging at a 90-degree angle to my wrist. I was driven to the Taber hospital, where they set the bone and put on a cast. After a couple of weeks, they noticed the bone was not healing correctly, so they had to re-break the bone and set it again.

I proudly wore my plaster medal of courage for two months before it was time to remove it. I am not saying that medicine in those days was medieval, but when they cut the cast off, they somehow ended up cutting the underside of my arm. To this day, on top of my arm, the 1-inch scar where they cut to set the bones has grown to about three inches in length, and on the bottom of my arm is a 4-inch scar line caused when they cut the cast off.

The worst part of all is that the bone never did set correctly, and I cannot turn my left-hand open. It makes it impossible for me to receive change after paying for something unless I use my right hand. It has also severely impacted my baseball and golf swings. This is probably the only reason I didn't make the major leagues as a Professional Baseball star or a Professional Golfer. That's my story, and I'm sticking to it.

The Spice of Life

As a Grade 1 student, my formal education began when I entered the hallowed halls of learning at the Chamberlain School in Grassy Lake. My mother taught Grade 2, and my Uncle Nick was the Principal. While most students attending school have the freedom of some anonymity, there was no trouble I got into at school that did not result in my getting into more trouble when I got home.

I attended Grades 1-9 in Grassy, and most of those years were typical for any normal small town boy. I must mention that my central claim to stardom came early on in my schooling career. It occurred in Grade 1, and while I did not sign with any major movie productions, I did get my 15 seconds of fame.

The Chamberlain High School had a vibrant drama club that involved students from grades seven through twelve. Each year, they spent months preparing for their blockbuster play's debut. The year was 1958, and I was an energetic young lad in Grade 1. I am not 100% sure of the presentation, but for some reason, "Alice in Wonderland" keeps popping up in my memory bank. At some point in the play, a cook was preparing a meal for the King and Queen, and the director required six small students who would play the part of different spices.

I was chosen to be the most special spice of all, that being *Cinnamon*. Our role involved us walking on stage, bringing our spices to the cook. I was the only spice that had the honour of "speaking."

I had three words to say, and while I don't remember exactly what they were, it was probably something like, "Don't forget me."

We all proudly marched onto the stage for our one-minute appearance. I flawlessly delivered my line, and the packed audience roared with laughter and rose to give a standing ovation. And then, we walked off the stage. This may not be exactly how the event occurred, but I have proof I was a part of the production.

At the end of the year, during the awards ceremony, I proudly walked to the front, along with the other cast members, and was presented with my tiny little trophy that only had one word engraved on it. If any of my offspring find a trophy with the inscription *Cinnamon* on it, that is how it came to be in my possession.

Where There's Smoke

There was not a lot for a kid growing up in Grassy Lake to do. There was the pool hall where my cousins Terence and Brian would take me to watch them play pool. Unfortunately, you had to be 16 to go in alone. The only other option was Moih's. It was a combination restaurant and convenience store. That meant it sold pretty much anything and everything you could ever need.

This place was right out of the movie *Happy Days*. There were numerous tables distributed around where you could sit and eat your hamburger and fries, along with your favourite milkshake. Each booth had an individual jukebox listing all the songs you could listen to for the cost of one nickel each. I was not old enough to have enough money to do this, but we always dreamed of the day we would be "cool" enough to sit there and visit and laugh, just like the big kids.

While you could buy the usual things such as candy bars and pop, there were some "secret" things that were also sold. You just had to know and ask about them because they were not publicly displayed. One of these items was mainly sold to the older boys. We had no idea what they were for; however once, in a while, one of the guys would give us one to play with. They would laugh like hyenas as we blew them up and ran home to show our parents the fantastic balloons.

The most exciting thing we could buy that wasn't displayed were "firecrackers." They included both the finger ones that came in packs of 25 and the enormous blockbusters, which were ten times more powerful. I couldn't count how many times these things would misfire early and explode while we were still holding them. While the burning sensation only lasted for a couple of minutes, the loud bang was enough to cause you to have an accident in your pants.

One day, our fun with firecrackers almost got us into big-time trouble. Billy, a friend, who ended up drowning not too long after this, and I walked east of Grassy towards the Turnbull farm. While we were walking through the field, we fired off our explosives collection. It wasn't until one of us turned around that we saw what we had started. The dry grass and weeds had caught fire, and there was a blaze spreading out in all directions.

I am not sure how we managed it, but we stamped on the flames and eventually put the fire out. Apparently, in the early 1900s, Grassy Lake was a thriving metropolis that ended up being wiped out by a fire started from the wheels of a passing locomotive. We were very fortunate not to be infamous as the cause of the second major fire in the town's history.

The Pinball Wizard

To say Grassy Lake was a small town would be an overstatement. It was so tiny that the phone book listed only the residents' first names. The total population was a whopping 276 people, give or take. It was the stereotypical Mayberry, where you knew everyone, and everyone knew you. It was the epitome of "It takes an entire village to raise a child."

As kids, we would leave the house after breakfast in the morning and sometimes not return until supper. Our parents generally knew who we were with because there weren't many kids in the town. However, they had no clue where we spent our time or what we were doing. It wasn't always a good thing, but generally, we didn't get into too much serious trouble.

Some of our favourite activities involved communing with nature. We would ride our bikes west of town to the nearest irrigation canal. This was our swimming pool as there was a small dam built to hold the water back. It was deep enough that we could jump and dive in. On the other side of this small dam was a culvert that ran underneath the highway. The opening was large enough for us to swim through.

The only hitch was that when it was full of water, it was impossible to stop for a breath of air along the way. While it was probably only about 25 feet long, it seemed like a mile to us. I can remember as I swam out the other end and broke the surface of the water, gulping for air and allowing my burning lungs to fill with oxygen.

If we biked North of town, it was only a short ride to the jungle. In reality, it was just a grove of poplar trees. These trees were ancient and tall, and the best thing was that the branches were perfect for climbing. With a bit of effort and agility, we scaled our imaginary Mount Everest. From 30 feet up in a tree, the experience of freedom and invulnerability is one of the best feelings imaginable.

My parents grew up in the 30s in Saskatchewan during the Great Depression. My mother told stories of travelers who would unexpectedly show up at their door, asking for a meal, and my grandparents would never turn them away without feeding them. No one had a lot of money in those days, and they learned how to be frugal. As kids, we never lacked food and clothing or other essentials, but we certainly didn't get everything we wanted.

To teach us the value of money, we did receive a weekly allowance. The earliest amount I can remember receiving was 25 cents/week. It may not sound like much, but in those days, you could buy candies that were five for a penny, chips and chocolate bars for 5 and 10 cents, and a pop for 12 cents. Our biggest dilemma was whether to space it out and buy a little each day or wait until the day before we got the next allowance and blow it all on pop and chips.

Even though the town was small, we had most of the conveniences. There were two general stores, an all-in-one gas station/garage/restaurant, a tavern, a pool hall, three wooden grain elevators, and a restaurant/soda bar. While we were not old enough to get a job, we quickly discovered ways to supplement our income. We became very proficient at learning the schedules of trucks and suppliers who delivered products to the town, and we got to know the drivers on a first-name basis.

One of my best friends was Ross. His parents owned the local Esso gas station, garage, and restaurant. This building is still standing and continues to be used as a restaurant today. We often ate at the restaurant. Mom disliked making lunches. She would set up a tab for us, and every school day, we would enjoy a lunch of hamburgers and fries. I never got tired of this, and to this day, I realize it was the best lunch any kid could ever dream of.

Attached to the restaurant was a garage where Ross's dad, Ken, would work on cars. Ken was never too busy to explain what he was doing to a particular vehicle. One thing he told me was forever ingrained into my memory banks. I can remember him saying how expensive it was to get their cars fixed. He commented that he didn't doubt someday people would have to pay over $20 each time they came in to get something fixed.

I talked earlier about Moih's café. This establishment housed the only two Pinball machines in town and the one Jukebox filled with 45 RPM vinyl records. We quickly became friends with the men who serviced these on a weekly basis.

Our two favourite days were Tuesday and Friday. On Tuesday, the Jukebox Man would come and swap out the records. The old ones he took out were still in great shape, just not the most current on the hit parade. The Jukebox Man taught us to barter. If we helped him carry things in and out to his car, we could generally negotiate a better deal when buying the records.

If we could time it, so we were there when he arrived, we would have the first pick of the selections he removed from the machine. The price generally started at 10 cents a record, but we could usually work him down to 5 cents through negotiation. He would allow us to buy as many as we could afford at that price. I remember the two records being my best purchases were "The Birds and the Bees" by Jewel Akens and "Crystal Chandelier" by Carl Belew. The thing we never realized until later was that the Jukebox Man would generally, on his way out, buy us a pop or some candy, so, in reality, we got the records and also got our money back in product. We did indeed learn the finer points of negotiation.

Friday was Pinball Man Day. He would either come in to change out one of the machines for a new one or check out the current ones to make sure they were still working well. One of the things he had to do was adjust the machine so it would tilt if lifted or pushed too hard. This ensured that we "Pinball Wizards" couldn't jar the game in a way that would give us an advantage and prolong the game. We became great helpers for him, and we imagined ourselves as essential servants he couldn't do without.

Whether he needed a screwdriver, pliers, or a wrench, we would make sure he got what he needed, immediately. Once the machines were serviced, the technician would load on some free games to test everything. Depending on his mood, he would always leave extra free games and walk away, telling us to enjoy ourselves. While the number of games that he left often varied, we still managed to snag enough to give us a couple of hours of free entertainment.

Abducted

As I said earlier, my best friend's parents owned the gas station in town. Monday was the day when our favourite supplier brought in his product. Since I don't remember his name, I will call him TMM, short for "The McGavin's Man." Anyone local knows McGavin's as a well-known bakery and distributor based in Lethbridge, that is still operating to this very day.

We thought TMM was the "Best." He was friendly, had a great sense of humour, and loved to tease us. The best part was there would often be a free donut or cupcake involved, and what kid could resist that. We were very helpful and volunteered to carry bread and other items into the store, hoping our reward would be one of the many tasty treats.

One day TMM asked me to jump into the back of his truck and bring out a couple of loaves of bread for him. I had just walked up to the bread pile when I heard the sound of the big sliding back door closing. When it locked into place, it was as if I were inside a mine, 400 feet below the surface. You couldn't see the hand in front of your face. I didn't have much time to react, as suddenly, the truck started up, and we were moving.

I don't remember being overly upset, but I remember wondering how I would get back home. In reality, the TMM had another delivery on the other side of town, so it was maybe a three-minute ride to the grocery store across the railroad tracks. When the truck stopped, and the door opened, the first thing I saw was TMM laughing as if he had just pulled the funniest prank ever. In the end, I received not one, but two treats in compensation for this prank.

There was no lasting harm done, and I am certain TMM had nothing but the best intentions of pulling a funny joke. However, can you imagine the consequences of an action such as that in today's world? My, how things have changed. Of course, I never told my parents. I was just happy to get a couple of free cupcakes.

In retrospect, the biggest lesson we learned was if you were respectful to people and willing to help them, you were generally rewarded in the end. And even if we didn't "get" something, we always felt better, thinking we had "helped." These lessons learned early on helped influence me positively throughout my life.

Old "Ouch" Potato Chips

In the 1960s, Old Dutch Potato Chips figured out a great way to market themselves. In conjunction with a Lethbridge television station, CJLH, they created a "Game Show" called *Kids' Bids*. It featured prizes children could bid on and win during a live auction. Prizes varied in value, but sometimes, to boost ratings, bicycles and other large items went up for auction.

The currency used to bid came in the form of empty bags and boxes of Old Dutch Potato Chips. The small bags of chips were worth 10 points each, the large bags were 15 points, and the boxes were a whopping 25 points. The bidders had to add up their totals, bundle them in groups, and have the empty wrappers available to cash in if they won the auction. There were rumors of scandals where unsavory kids would stuff their boxes full of newspaper, claiming to have legitimate Old Dutch bags stuffed inside. Unfortunately, I was never smart enough to think of those things.

Once I reached the ripe old age of 10, my parents agreed they would drive me to Lethbridge to be on television if I could collect enough points. Living in a small town and knowing everyone there had its advantages. It wasn't long before everyone in town was saving their Old Dutch bags and boxes for me. I would make a weekly round to every household, and sometimes I had to gently chastise people if they hadn't eaten their expected quota of chips. While I never had to break any kneecaps, the message always got across.

For weeks, every Saturday morning was spent glued to the television, watching Bob Lang, the show's emcee, as he gave away prizes, I could only fantasize about. I vividly recall one kid from Lethbridge who was on the show every week. He either knew every person in Lethbridge, or his dad owned Old Dutch Foods. He always had enough "cash" to buy the biggest and best of the prizes. Today, looking back, he must have had "mafia" connections.

After several months of berating my neighbours for not eating enough junk food, I had managed to collect enough points that I at least had a chance of being a successful bidder on some of the prizes. I had carefully sorted the wrappers into stacks of "1000 points" each. When Saturday finally arrived, we packed up my entire collection of points, and in less than an hour, we were parking the car and entering the television studios. As we walked into the room, I will never forget how it looked so different from on television. It was a tiny little space with equipment and "technical junk" scattered everywhere. On the television, it looked like the show was produced and filmed inside a spacious and finely appointed castle.

My worst fears were quickly realized when I looked around, and there HE was. My "Arch Nemesis," "Mister, I got more points than anyone else alive." He was sitting a couple of seats down from me. Why couldn't he have come down with something like the bubonic plague that would have prevented him from once again dominating the bidding action? I don't remember much about the auction, except I finally was able to win a prize, not one of the bicycles, mind you. It was a football helmet that I might grow into in several years. It didn't matter. All I cared about was that I wasn't going home empty-handed. I did get to go up to the front, where Bob Lang did a short interview with me. It was my first introduction to "Stardom." While it probably only lasted a few seconds, I was mentally practicing how I would tell all the people lined up to get my autograph, to be patient as I would get to them, eventually.

I did get proof of my appearance on television as my Uncle Nick had the old-style movie projector that took two people to lift. He captured my debut by filming the show from home off the television screen. While the quality was not quite "High Definition," you could make out a few of my features if you squinted. I would pay a lot of money to have a copy of that video today, but alas, there were probably many weddings and birthday parties copied over it throughout the years.

To this day, I have flashbacks whenever I see the Old Dutch logo. I hope one day I will grow into that football helmet. Kudos to Old Dutch for being ahead of their time and encouraging us, as children, to recycle.

In case you are perplexed by the title, let me explain. If you look at the Old Dutch Logo on any bag of chips, you will see it has a very stylized font. If you read over it quickly, as I usually did, there is no question the D in Dutch looks more like an O, thereby explaining the confusion.

The Child Prodigy

Appearing on *Kids' Bids* was not my only foray into the entertainment business. Not many people are aware that at an early age, I displayed an artistic flair for music. My parents convinced me an accordion was a much sexier instrument than a guitar or drums, and if I practiced hard, who knows, a group like the Beatles might pick me up. I would refer to my accordion as my secret "Chick Magnet" with that thought in mind. At the time, I did not realize the only chicks an accordion attracts are at least 70 years old.

In those days, there was a major event called the Kiwanis Music Festival, where aspiring musicians could compete and show the world how talented they were. There were only the contestants and their parents in the audience. Against my better judgment, my accordion teacher, Mr. Galloway, entered me in the local competition in Lethbridge.

I practiced for weeks, and soon I could play the "Beer Barrel Polka" without having to look at the music. I was confident it was a lock that I would easily win the competition and go on to bigger and better things. I had visions of touring Germany during Octoberfest and filling arenas with thousands of screaming fans.

When the day of the festival came, I was READY to bring a smile to the face of every *fraulein* in Lethbridge. I can remember sitting in the audience in an aisle chair with my accordion strapped tightly to my chest. We had to be wearing the accordion beforehand to help speed things along.

When my name was finally called, I remember standing up and walking towards the stage. The next thing I remember is falling forward and sliding head-first on the floor with the accordion cushioning my fall. Let me correct that. It hurt like hell to land on that stupid, hard instrument. In the end, the only thing injured was my pride. Other than a few skid marks on the accordion, damages were minimal. I did manage to pull myself together and play the song, although I never did hear from any scouts or rock bands in need of an Accordion Aficionado.

Who knows, without that fall from grace, I could have been the next Weird Al Yankovic or maybe even have appeared along with Don Messer or Lawrence Welk.

The Proof is in the Pudding

Old Dutch bags were the start of my collecting career but not its end. I immediately moved on to Jello Pudding. It started with the company inserting one round disk featuring early cars inside each package. There were 250 cars in total, going back to the earliest horseless carriages. There was also a round carousel that kept the disks safely stored. It could be purchased, through the mail, by sending in money and box tops. I am not sure how much pudding Mom bought and made, but we didn't stop until I had completed my entire collection of cars.

Of course, we often got doubles, so I also learned about bartering and negotiating at an early age. I can remember Mom saying she hoped I would soon finish the collection. We could finally get a break from eating pudding. Being the shrewd marketers they were, surprise, surprise, they decided to print a set of airplanes. I am not sure if there were any other series produced after that. By the time I completed the airplane edition, everyone in our family had started to resemble pudding.

These two sets were my pride and joy, and I spent countless hours rearranging them and admiring the beauty of each disk. I didn't know it at the time, but someday they would be worth a great deal of money. That is, if they were kept in pristine condition. My mother, the eternal educator, had discovered these disks were perfect for teaching math skills to her Grade 1 students.

The disks had been produced, so #1-25 were purple, 26-50 were red, and so on up to 250. Mom discovered if she glued strips of magnets to the disk's face, they would stick to the blackboard, coloured side out. The students could add or subtract these by moving them on the blackboard. This was the first and very primitive "Smartboard."

One day, I can remember visiting home and asking Mom about my pudding wheels. I had discovered that early collections of things, such as baseball and hockey cards, had become very valuable. I was sure I had a priceless collector set, with carousel included, that I could sell for hundreds of dollars.

When I saw my treasured cars with magnets glued to them, my heart fell. When I tried to take the magnet off, all that was left was a torn picture underneath. My priceless treasure was sunk. On a positive note, I am sure many former Grade 1 students out there owe their math skills to me and my collection. Perhaps if they all donated a few bucks, I could recoup my investment.

Just Scraping By

The first car I remember my dad owning was a 1956 Blue and White Chevy "Bel-Air." At Christmas, our parents would pack up the car to go back to Saskatchewan to visit the grandparents. Mom would place the suitcases on the floor between the back seat and the front seats. She would pile quilts on top, and we ended up with a bed in the back, where we could sleep during the trip.

Some of you are probably wondering about seat belts and children's car seats. We didn't even know if the car had seat belts in those days. I can't remember the first time I wore a seat belt. However, I remember riding on the shelf above the back seat just under the rear windshield.

Other trips involved traveling to Winnipeg to visit Uncle Bill and Aunt Lil (Mom's sister). We used to leave at 4:00 in the morning so we kids could sleep for a few hours before we got too restless. The last trip we took in the Chevy was the most memorable. We only made it as far as Piapot, Saskatchewan, which was barely a couple of hours from home. The car broke down, and we had to spend the better part of the day there, getting it fixed. When we finally did get to Winnipeg, the first thing Dad did was to go out and buy a new car. It was a GORGEOUS 1961 jet-black Ford Fairlane 500 with big fins on the back. It was a thing of beauty. I would kill to have that car today.

This car served us well for quite a few years. Unfortunately, I was the only one who ever did any detailing on the vehicle. I will never forget that day. Dad would let me drive the car back and forth in our driveway. To practice, I would back it up and then go forward. Sometimes I would do this for hours. I am not sure if it racked up any miles on the odometer. When you go in reverse, does the mileage come off? If so, the total result would have been zero.

One day I believed I was ready to step up to the next level. Previously, Dad had backed the car out of the garage into the driveway. I wanted to practice driving this day, but the car was still in the garage. I decided I didn't need help with backing it out. This was something an experienced backer-upper, like myself, could handle. It was a narrow one-car garage, with not a lot of room on either side. I remember about halfway out, thinking I was getting pretty close to the drivers' side. I turned the wheels hard, and the next thing I heard was the front of the car scrapping as it passed by the garage door.

I remember getting out and gasping at what I saw. The beautiful black paint had been scraped off, and you could see the shiny silver metal underneath. Dad never did fix the marks, so they were always there to remind me of how NOT to backup. I don't remember being punished for this, but I doubt they could have ever made me feel worse than I already felt when it happened. To this day, I am meticulous when I back up. With today's backup cameras and side warning alarms, no child should ever have to endure that kind of cruel and inhumane punishment again.

A Little Off the Top

The local businesses in Grassy Lake were able to supply most of our daily necessities of life. However, we still had to travel to the city a couple of times a month to satisfy some of our more eclectic creature comforts. Saturday was always travel day. Since it was a good half-hour trip, we would tend to make a full day of it each way. Once lunch had been consumed, and the dishes were done, we all jumped into the car and headed for the "bright lights" of Taber Town.

Knowing we wouldn't be home until well past dark, Dad had to prepare the car's back seat in advance. He made a reasonably level surface by putting some boxes between the seats. Mom would spread a thick wool quilt on top, and the result was a king-sized car bed, perfect for three sleepy kids.

Once we got to Taber, we would park somewhere along Main Street and head our separate ways. Mom and my sisters would go off shopping, and I got to go with Dad. We, of course, went off to do "guy" things. While we would generally do a little shopping in the McLeods Hardware Store, I knew it wouldn't be long before we ended up at my favourite place in the whole world.

I am talking about the place where "Real Men" hung out. Looking back, I would have to say it was a precursor to the modern-day internet café. Not that there was any food or drink sold or purchased. This was where all the local, national, and international news of the world was discussed. There were always five or six "old" (at least

30-40 years old) men sitting around either learning or pontifying as to how they could solve all the problems of the world.

In case you haven't guessed yet, I am talking about our bi-monthly visit to the Barber Shop. My dad sported a trendy "brush cut." All the hair on top of his head was trimmed to about ¾ of an inch and shaped flat. It resembled an upside-down brush with all the hairs standing straight up. If I'm not mistaken, he paid a total of 2-bits (25 cents) for this particular style of grooming. Once in a while, Dad would splurge and get a shave as well. I was never sure what special occasion necessitated his spending an extra 10 cents for a shave. I guess, sometimes, even "Real Men" need a little pampering.

Once Dad was finished, it was my turn. When I would walk up to the chair, the barber was already reaching for the booster seat he would place across the center, so I sat up higher in the chair. I HATED that seat because it was a stark reminder, I was still a "little kid," and what kid didn't dream of being a "big kid." Unfortunately, I WAS small for my age, and the booster seat was always a part of the routine.

There finally came a day when I was officially inducted into the Hall of Manhood. As I walked towards the barber, I noticed he wasn't reaching for the booster. He held his hand to the level of the top of my head and looked at the barber chair. He nodded his head and then helped me up to the regular seat, where I plunked my butt down and proudly held my head up high. It was one of those "defining" moments in a person's life.

The regular patrons were there, not only for a haircut but to visit and give all the kids a hard time. The barber loved to tease as much as anyone. One day he decided it would be funny to provide me with a "shave." I was probably still using the booster seat, but when he told me to stroke my chin and asked me if I needed a shave, I could swear I felt a little stubble.

I remember the barber getting the cup that held the solid shaving soap in it. He took one of those horsehair brushes with an oversized ivory handle and dabbed it in hot water, and swirled it around in the cup. It wasn't long before there was a thick head of foam in the cup. He used the brush to dab the foam on my chin and cheeks. As he turned me around to look at myself in the giant mirror behind us, I am not sure who had the bigger smile on their face, him or me. He took out the long straight razor, and using the blunt backside, proceeded to scrape the foam off. Once I was cleaned up, he splashed on some aftershave, and I was good to go. And best of all, he didn't even charge Dad the extra 10 cents.

The Show Must Go On

Our weekly trip to the city featured a couple of routines that were non-negotiable. Once all the shopping was complete, it was off to Sparky's Drive-In. McDonald's or any of the other fast-food chains had not yet been invented. Sparkys occupied the exact spot where the A & W is today. I am sure Sparkys had a full menu, but the only thing our family ever ordered was the fish and chips. If memory serves me well, they were the BEST fish and chips in the whole wide world.

Once our bellies were filled, it was time to head to another Drive-In. This being the Drive-Inn Movie Theatre, located a mile West of Town, alongside the highway. While the primary intent was to view an exciting first-run movie, there was an ulterior motive for us kids. The film couldn't start until it was dark, but we would always arrive a couple of hours early. This would give us plenty of time to get out and play with all the other kids.

It didn't matter that you didn't know anyone. During that time, free from adult supervision, you were best buddies with complete strangers. There were swings, a slide, and a teeter-totter. If these were busy, there were all kinds of great places to play hide and seek. It was always a bittersweet moment when the projector would start, and we would have to find our way back to the car. Since we had eaten before arriving at the Drive-Inn, we never visited the concession stand until the intermission, after the first movie.

For those unfamiliar with drive-inns, there were always two movies shown, along with many cartoons that were not available on television. The first movie was usually an older movie we had all previously seen, but can you ever get enough of watching a classic Western over and over?

In the comfort of our vehicle, there we were listening to a speaker we brought inside the car and hooked on to the window. I wouldn't say it produced a high-fidelity stereophonic sound. It was more crackling and hissing, but it was the sweetest sound imaginable to our ears. I wonder how many of these speakers were ripped out or windows were broken by people forgetting to replace the speaker outside at the end of the movie.

The second movie was the feature movie. This meant it was time for our usual trek to the concession stand. There was no smell like that which greeted you as you entered the most fabulous place in the world. Disneyland had nothing over that place. To this day, the aroma of fresh-popped popcorn is something that floods my memory banks. We would get a couple of big bags of popcorn and a couple of large cokes to share. If Dad was in a generous mood, we might even get a chocolate bar.

Since we were so young, I didn't understand all of the drive-inn format's nuances. On the trip back from the concession, I remember asking Dad why some of the car windows were all fogged up, and there were two people "wrestling" in the backseat with no one sitting in the front. Dad, who was never a man of many words, would smile and shrug his shoulders. It would be interesting to know how many of us were conceived during a trip to the Drive-Inn Theatre.

Not Even the
Red Cross Wants Me

My favourite expression regarding the accumulation of "scars" during our lifetimes references the fact, "You have to be alive to get scars." Some people wear their childhood scars with pride and use them to remind themselves that if it doesn't kill you, it makes you stronger. I prefer the description," Scars are tattoos with better stories."

Many people purposely submit themselves to hours of pain at the cost of thousands of dollars to scar their bodies. They believe this "body art" makes them more beautiful and, more importantly, highlights their individualism. The two most common methods of art are tattoos and branding.

The most bizarre tattoo I have ever seen covered the entire back of a young lady in her early 20s. She proudly displayed it as she was waitressing in a golf course restaurant. The tattoo included all the lyrics to Led Zeppelin's "Stairway to Heaven." I was amazed someone so young had even heard of Led Zeppelin.

I have always held a bizarre fascination with the detail and colour of some of the tattoos I have seen. It is not that I have never thought about getting a tattoo, but instead, there two little things preventing it. They are called "pain and needles."

The first time I remember being so deathly afraid of needles occurred in school when the nurse would come around and give us the various vaccinations. In those days, vaccinations were mandatory. To avoid getting "shot," I tried several different evasive techniques. Hiding out in the bathroom or down where the caretaker kept his supplies did prolong the agony for a few more minutes. However, ultimately, I was located and held down to receive the injection.

It was not until entering adulthood I realized how significant my aversion to pain and needles was. I remember convincing Irene it was our duty to be good citizens and donate our blood during one of the many blood drives held frequently. We both went to the clinic, and they put us in separate rooms. I had friends who had previously told me this was a relatively painless experience. I am not sure if they were lying or if perhaps, I was unlucky enough to get a nurse who put a very dull needle into the wrong spot.

As soon as she put the needle in and blood started to fill the bag, the intense pain began. I felt the throbbing with each heartbeat as my blood was pumping out of my body. I began to sweat, and the last thing I remembered was asking the nurse if this should be hurting so much.

The next thing I remember is opening my eyes with a cold compress on my forehead. My body was soaked in sweat, and I will never forget the panicked look on the nurse's face. The advice she gave me has lasted to this day. She told me I should NEVER give blood again. I tried to keep my sense of humour and asked her if they had at least taken out several bags of blood while I was unconscious. It was pretty embarrassing having to explain to Irene why it took me a half-hour longer than her to donate.

Later in life, I learned it was not only needles that made me faint. The same result could occur simply by watching movies with people suffering in pain. The first time such an incident occurred was during a film called *Clockwork Orange*. While the bad guy was being tortured, they had clamped his eyes open so he couldn't blink or look away. I started to feel queasy in the stomach and told Irene I was going to the bathroom. The next thing I remembered was waking up, laying on the floor in the bathroom with some stranger bending over me, asking me what I was "on."

The other movie which resulted in an unexpected, short snooze was *The Exorcist*. I will never forget when Linda Blair's head spun around like a top. By then, Irene was aware of my disposition to fainting, so I had strict orders NOT to go to the bathroom if I felt weak. We never did see the end of the movie as we left as soon as I regained consciousness. So, unless they come up with a tattooing method that involves no needles or pain, I will not be getting any ink work done soon.

Blowing Smoke
Out of Your Ears

The other form of body art I referenced previously is called branding. This involves taking thin wires or probes and heating them to burn the design into the flesh. This is definitely not something I would ever voluntarily submit to. Unfortunately, I have a branding design that I acquired in the seventh grade, though not through my own volition.

When you live in a small town, you tend to hang around with friends, both older and younger than yourself. That was because there were not many friends available. Unfortunately, not all of my friends were "good" friends. For whatever reason, I was hanging out with a couple of high school "friends," who shall forever remain nameless. One of them asked if I wanted to see him blow smoke out of his ears. Yes, they were smoking, and no, I was not.

He told me to go behind him and wrap my arms tightly around his waist. He said when I squeezed hard, and he took a puff of the cigarette, smoke would come out of his ears. What happened next was that he took his cigarette and, using the lit end of the cigarette, stuck it into the top of my hand.

He had my arms locked around him so that I couldn't pull away. I can still remember the pain as he held the cigarette to my hand and could feel the skin melting away. After what seemed like forever, he let my arms go. The two of them laughed as I screamed in pain. When I looked at the top of my right hand, I saw a perfect circle, the shape of a cigarette, burned into my flesh.

I am not sure how long the pain lasted, but this was not the worst part of the experience. I was faced with the prospect of making sure my parents did not see the scar as they would have assumed, I had been smoking.

It did not occur to me to tell them the truth and that it wasn't my fault. As anyone who has been bullied or abused knows, for some reason, whether it is fear of retribution or the unspoken code of silence, you don't implicate the perpetrators.

I can remember going home and putting a Band-Aid on, but I am not sure how I managed to keep this hidden from my parents. Maybe they knew but never asked. Every day, when I look at this scar, I remember wondering how anybody in their right mind could think it was funny to do something like that to another person.

Down in the Dumps

Parents, these days, would cringe if they found out their children were shopping in the world's earliest Costco. As a child, we spent countless hours perusing the various items on display and free for the taking. Just like any major big-box outlet, there were areas where you could find electronics, food items, appliances, and often mystery sections, where you never knew what you might score. If you haven't guessed by now, I am talking about the wonderland of discarded items, known as the Grassy Lake Garbage Dump.

The dump was only a short bike ride out of town, and once there, we could spend hours exploring and looking for buried treasure. We would often find riches we could proudly take home to enjoy later. The "Holy Grail" we were always looking for were the discarded aerosol cans. While we never had the guts to try to light one as a torch, we completely understand what it meant by contents under pressure and keep away from heat. When we were able to score one of these cans, especially those that were not completely empty, we would store them in a secret cache that we would access later.

It seemed about once a month, individual sections of the dump were set on fire to reduce the volume of waste. Burn day was our "ABC" day. While for adult males, ABC stands for Anniversary, Birthday, and Christmas, to us, it meant, Aerosol Bomb Cans.

We would position ourselves a "safe" distance away from the fire to practice our aim with our primitive grenades. We would pretend to "pull the pin" with our mouths, count to three, and throw the cans over our heads into the fire. A short while later, we were rewarded with a bomb blast that resulted in the can being shot upwards into the air. I can still picture us dug into our trenches and slowing down the advancing enemy lines as we peppered them with our deadly explosives. In the end, we won the war and lived to fight another day.

I can visualize many of you cringing at us scavenging through the garbage, exposing our tender young bodies to all strains of bacteria and disease. You have to realize, as kids, we also drank from garden hoses and licked off each other's ice cream cones and popsicles. I don't remember being sick often, so we probably had some pretty effective immune systems. I doubt that the current World Health Organization would approve of such unsanitary behaviours.

Going to the dump was also sometimes a family activity. Anyone who spent time visiting and camping in Waterton Lakes Park probably spent at least part of a day visiting the dump grounds there. Although this was not on the Visitor's Guide, as far as exciting things to do, in and around Waterton, locals regarded this as a "Must See." We would sit in the car and watch as the bears would wander around, searching for food. If you were lucky, there would be several bears scavenging through the refuse. I was always hopeful we would spot Yogi or Booboo in person one of those times. It sometimes resembled a Drive-Inn Theatre, with all the cars parked, watching the feature attraction.

It seems over the years, they have realized how valuable these dumping grounds are. They have enclosed them with tall fences that are kept locked unless the armed guard at the gate is on duty. Whenever I get the opportunity to visit and make a drop-off, I still feel the urge to hunt around and look underneath things that are just lying around, waiting to be explored. It reminds me of shopping in Mexico when the aggressive salespeople tell you to come in and buy something you don't need.

Bless Me, Father, For I Have Sinned

For most of my early years, the church was not a big part of our lives. We might occasionally attend a service at Christmas time, and if memory serves, the church of choice was Lutheran. My mom had grown up as a Greek Orthodox Catholic, so when they decided it was important for our family to be exposed to some kind of faith, the chosen religion was Roman Catholic.

There was a Catholic Church in Grassy Lake, and at the time, there was a very charismatic young priest by the name of Father Lynn. Once my parents decided to join the church, he became a regular Friday night visitor. It would start with supper at our place, followed by religious sessions which involved our parents only. After several weeks, it came time for Dad's baptism. Since Mom was already a Catholic, she was exempt. Usually, the parents attend their children's baptism; however, we were able to attend and participate in his.

It was not long before Sunday Mass was a fixed part of our weekly schedule. Once Dad was baptized, it was time for the three children to follow. We attended Catechism, after school, for what seemed like a million weeks until we were ready for our "big day." The age for being able to participate in Communion is around seven years. It was decided that everything would be combined for us. On one day, we would get the entire "full meal deal" consisting of both Baptism and Communion.

It is worthy to note that in those days, the majority of the mass was done in Latin since the religion had its foundation in Rome. In Catechism, we had to learn all the different, appropriate responses that were recited aloud during mass. Much of this was in Latin. Not only did we have to learn about the bible, but we also had to learn a new language.

The most significant change to our lives involved the addition of fasting on Fridays. Eating meat on Friday was "verboten." The only protein we were allowed was fish. Most of the time, we were very faithful in this regard. However, once in a while, mainly if we were on holiday, we would forget that the day was Friday. Once we had finished our barbequed burgers, the shock of our "sinning" would strike us. We knew the only way to be saved was to admit our indiscretion the next time we went to confession.

Confession was the "biggie" for being a good Catholic. We were expected, every month; weekly, if we were extra naughty, to tell the priest all of the sins we had committed. We would receive the penance as to what it would take to absolve us from evil. Usually, the penance was in the form of many prayers that had to be recited after the confession was complete. It was always fun to go early, to sit in the pews, and watch the congregation going in and out of the confessional. Once they left the Confessional to kneel and begin the penance, I could time how long it took them to finish praying. In my mind, the longer they had to pray, the more sins they had committed. It was pretty easy to spot who the "big sinners" of the community were.

In those days, the Confessional was composed of an area that had thin partitions separating it into three small rooms. The priest sat in the middle, and the parishioners would enter either of the two remaining cubicles and kneel. It was pitch black inside the cubicle, giving us a false sense of anonymity. When the small door you spoke through was opened, you were reassured the priest could not see who you were. Of course, with him knowing the entire congregation, he immediately recognized your voice.

One of the hardest things was knowing it could be anyone in the room on the other side, even one of your parents. If you spoke too loudly, they, as well as the priest, could hear every sin you admitted to. When the priest opened the door, the confessor had to declare, "Bless me, Father, for I have sinned." This was always the best test to make sure you weren't speaking too loudly. If the priest had to ask you to repeat it, you knew it was the correct volume.

The tricky part of making your confession was deciding the order of the sins to be confessed. Even though at such young ages, the sins were never as exciting as murder or adultery, some of our indiscretions were worse than others. You did not want to start with a doozy right off the bat. You also did not want to wait until the very end to talk about the "big" ones. These were when I believed the priest was most focused and listening intently.

Not only did you have to admit sin, but you also had to tell how many times you committed the transgression. I would try to start with some of the basic ones like, "I disobeyed my parents 89 times". After three or four lame sins, I would throw in the one I hoped he would miss. Usually, it involved admitting to having lustful thoughts about girls. As an adolescent boy, what else did you think about?

The trick was to put it out there, almost as an afterthought, and quickly move on to the next trivial sin. I always hoped if I kept talking, he might forget the one I was trying to avoid responsibility for. However, as soon as I would stop to take a breath, the priest would interrupt. He would ask me to repeat the last sin to discuss it in detail. I was "busted." He would go on and on with the lecture about how it was "normal to have these feelings," but he would add that we must learn to control them. We seemed to have the same talk every week. You would think he would have understood the futility of his efforts.

I am reminded of the story where the young lad goes into the confessional and admits to being with a girl and getting to "second base." The priest immediately stops him and asks, "Was this with Helen?" The boy replies, "no, Father, it wasn't Helen." Well then was it with Mary and again the boy says no. After the priest makes a couple more guesses, the boy says, "I'm sorry, Father, I can't tell you who it was, but thanks for the great leads."

Service with a Smile

I feel it is necessary to preface the following comments by saying it is NOT my intent to make fun of my faith, but rather to point out how it sometimes appeared to a child's eyes. I am proud to call myself a Catholic and would not want anything I say to be construed as sacrilegious.

For those who are not familiar with the Catholic faith, Altar Boys were and still are, except now they can be "Altar Persons," considered an integral part of the celebration of mass. Their role is to act as the priest's assistant and do the little things that help the process go smoothly.

The beauty of the Catholic mass is that it is a very consistent form of worship. Every action and prayer are standardized and repeated each week. You can go from one Catholic church to another, anywhere in the world, and still follow what is going on, even if it is offered in a different language. To a child, it can sometimes become a little mechanical and rote. As an Altar Server, you had to be careful not to go on autopilot because if you missed one of your duties, everyone in the congregation knew it.

Whenever I have taken non-Catholic friends with me to the mass, they are most surprised by the physical workout you get. Throughout the hour of service, you stand, you sing, you sit, you listen, you kneel, you pray, then you repeat, many times. It is no wonder many Catholic athletes make the sign of the cross before and after a competition. Their weekly physical endurance training has well prepared them for their athletic accomplishments.

The one thing I always wonder about is if there are more than one of the athletes praying before their event, is it the one with the least number of sins who ends up getting the nod from above to be the winner? And what about those poor athletes who do not call for external help? Are they penalized and do not have a chance of victory, regardless of their preparation and training?

Many of the earlier traditions of the mass have changed, and there is one, in particular, I do not miss. It used to be customary for the priest to begin by walking down the aisle to bless the congregation. He would dip an aspergillum into a bucket of water and shake the holy water out overtop of the parishioners. If you happened to look up at the wrong time, there was a good chance you might get a spray of water in your face. It was incredibly frustrating if you wore glasses. My mother always insisted you could not wipe "holy water" off, and we had to endure our dirty lenses until we got out of the church.

As an Altar Boy, I always enjoyed the preparation before mass. We were charged with lighting all the many candles that were a part of the experience. What kid doesn't like to light things on fire? I can remember the feeling of power as hundreds of people watched while I took my time to strike the match and hover it over the wick until it burst into flame. And no one got upset at me for playing with fire.

The other thing was that before mass, we had to prepare the wine and the host. The wine had to be poured from the gallon container into the gold chalice that would be consecrated for consumption at the end of the service. We all knew you didn't dare mess with the holy wine. However, the wine that was in the big bottle was not blessed, and once in a while, we could not resist the temptation to sneak a sample. In all honesty, I hated the taste, which helped limit my consumption. When I think back, any time you buy your wine in the economy-sized jug, we are not talking about a fine wine with a particular bouquet or vintage.

It was always interesting whenever a visiting priest would have to fill in for our regular parish priest. Usually, these were extremely elderly, retired priests who were on call to help out in the case of sickness or when the local priest went on vacation. They tended to have short fuses when it came to their patience levels. Now that I have reached the same age they were, I understand why they sometimes reacted the way they did.

One of our big jobs was to bring the chair for the priest to sit on while the lectors did the reading. After the lector had finished, it was time for the priest to read. We were responsible for taking the chair away. Sometimes, my thoughts would wander to what I would be doing later that day, and I would forget to remove the chair. You knew you were in trouble when the priest picked the chair up and threw it towards you. You made sure the next time you were taking the chair away, even before he was getting up.

The least favourite masses I served were on those special occasions called "High Mass." These happened on the most sacred days and also at funerals. This was the only time when they pulled out the incense. Our job was to hold the "thurible," which was suspended by chains and housed the incense. It would be lit by the priest, and the altar boy held it in preparation for its use to consecrate the altar. If the priest happened to take a little longer to start the process, we would end up engulfed in a haze of smoke. It was not unheard of for Altar Boys to pass out from the smell. While I never succumbed to the fumes, it was excellent training for a future as a firefighter.

One of the most bizarre events I can remember as an Altar Boy was the first time that I served a wedding ceremony. It was an honour to be asked by the happy couple to help out on this special occasion. Plus, you knew there would be a special envelope handed to you at the end that would usually contain a $5 bill. That was more than I made in a month doing anything else.

The local priest at this time was relatively new at the job and still learning the tricks of the trade. I will never forget the murmur that started going through the congregation as he read from the bible. He seemed a little flustered but was too embarrassed to stop. The various scripture readings are separated by long ribbons that the priest uses to mark their place. Somehow, he had opened up to the wrong section and read the text, typically used at a funeral. This was a little more memorable than any of us had wanted to experience. Much later after, we laughed about this, and it never got old, reminding Father about the incident.

As a teenager, your enthusiasm for the church sometimes tends to wane. We were fortunate to have some younger priests who had a knack for relating to us and keeping us involved with the church. I remember going on overnight camping trips to Calgary, where we visited the Happy Valley recreation center. Our priest had access to a stretch limo which someone in Milk River had built and put in five rows of seats. It was a real surprise when we would pull up in front of a movie theatre, and 15 of us would jump out, just like we were heading on to the "Red Carpet" at the Oscars.

We were very fortunate to have had so many amazing priests, who we were proud to call friends. When they would drop by unexpectedly for supper, it was considered an honour to host them. They were considered an integral part of the community.

Back to School

When I was born, my parents lived with my grandparents on a small farm located several miles out of Runnymede, Saskatchewan. My mother taught school in a one-room schoolhouse located on a lot adjacent to our farmhouse. It did not take my dad long to realize this was not a sustainable arrangement for raising a family. Even with Mom's teaching salary, the amount of land they farmed would barely provide basic life necessities.

My Mom's brother-in-law, Uncle Nick, who was also a teacher, was responsible for our moving to Alberta. He took the principalship in Grassy Lake and told my parents there were jobs there for both of them. Mom was hired as a Grade 2 teacher, and Dad got a job working with the Water Resources, which today is known as the Saint Mary River Irrigation Development or SMRID for short. Dad's job was operating a Uke. This was an abbreviation for Euclid, which was a monster earth mover. These enormous machines could quickly excavate large amounts of dirt and rock.

The ride in these machines was bumpier than anything you would find in a ride at an exhibition. The constant bouncing over several years resulted in various back complications which came close to crippling Dad. I remember visiting him in the hospital after a severe back spasm. He was in "traction," which meant he was flat on his back, and his legs were elevated and suspended by ropes and pulleys, trying to stretch muscles and ligaments to relieve his pain. It was not long after that the pain became so bad, he had to switch careers.

Dad's back was not his only serious health issue. There was another time when he was injured while they were pounding metal posts into the ground. Dad held the rod while the other fellow used a sledgehammer to strike the top of the post. During one of the swings, a sharp sliver of steel flew off and caught my dad in the upper thigh. He immediately started to bleed like the "proverbial stuffed pig." They rushed him to the Taber Hospital, which was about a half-hour away. By the time they got to see a doctor, the steel shard had entered the bloodstream and disappeared. The doctor was worried the results would be catastrophic if it entered the heart.

Dad was kept overnight and it wasn't until the next day that they finally located the steel. Fortunately for Dad, it had lodged in his lungs and was impacted there. The doctor decided the risk of removing it was far worse than just leaving it where it was and letting the body heal over it. Every year, after, he would get an x-ray that would clarify if the sliver was still safely lodged in place.

Once Dad realized he could no longer drive large equipment, he decided to pursue the one thing he had always dreamed of doing. He was a magician with tools and loved to tinker on anything mechanical. With his talented hands, he could fix or build anything. If you wonder if this was passed on to me, the answer is a definite NO. The only talent I have with anything mechanical is that I can always manage to "screw" it up. The "build it" gene skipped a generation, and our son inherited it.

To become a certified mechanic, Dad began a two-year stint, attending SAIT in Calgary. He enrolled in the Diesel Mechanic program, which involved fixing large equipment. For two years, my mother, two sisters, and I lived in Grassy Lake while he "board and roomed" in a basement suite on 16th Ave in Calgary.

He would get up at 4:00 am every Monday and drive to Calgary, where he would immediately go to class. After his last class on Friday afternoon, he would commute the 3.5 hours back and usually be home before our bedtime. He did this EVERY week of those two years, and it was always a sad Sunday night when we knew he would once again leave us the following day.

The thing I remember most about his further education experience was how much homework my mother had to do. With any of the practical assignments, Dad could weld, take apart, and fix anything they threw at him. However, sometimes he had to do things like write book reports. This was not his forte. So, I can remember my mother, and I read "The Call of the Wild" together, and then Mom wrote the report to be ready for Dad when he came home on the weekend.

He ended up completing the course, book reports, and all and had no trouble finding his dream job. He was immediately hired to work at International Harvester in Burdett. After several years, the dealership moved to Bow Island, and soon after, so did our family. The ironic thing is I have come full circle, and we are now living in the same house we moved to when we first came to Bow Island in 1967.

Shell Shocked

My father was a Grade 5 graduate. He quit school at the ripe old age of 11 to stay home and help out on the farm. From the stories Dad told us about his schooling, I realize I did acquire some of his genes when it came to finding ways to annoy teachers. I am reasonably confident that when he announced to the teacher he would not be returning to class, there was not much trying to change his mind.

The only time he could be accused of being the teacher's pet was when he married the teacher. He told one story, in particular, that he was most proud of sharing. There was a test they were going to be writing, and somehow he had forgot to do any studying for it. He figured if he could cause a distraction, there might be a way to prolong the agony of having to write the test.

In those days, the teacher was responsible for all caretaking duties, along with the teaching responsibilities. The teacher had to come in early to start the fire in the stove so the schoolroom would be heated for the students when they arrived. Students were assigned many of the caretaking tasks, and one of these was to bring wood in and keep the fire stoked in the potbelly stove at the back of the room.

Dad figured out the perfect crime. He volunteered to take care of the fire for the day, which would allow him access to the stove, at the appropriate time. When it was getting close to the time to write the test, he went to the back of the room, where the stove was located.

Students, in those days, used to bring their guns (22 caliber rifles) to school because you never knew when you might spot some game to shoot along the way. Amazingly enough, with all the thousands of guns brought to school daily, there was not one recorded mass shooting that occurred. Is it possible the current problems are not the fault of the "guns"? But I digress.

Dad took several 22 shells and threw them into the fire before running back to his desk. He calculated that when the shells exploded, it would scare everyone, and they would have to clear out the school. The plan worked perfectly as the bullets made a loud bang when they exploded. Fortunately, no one was injured by the flying lead, and it did not take a lot of interrogation before the teacher was able to determine the culprit.

I believe the punishment resulted in his not being able to sit down for several hours, and in the end, he still had to write the test. I do not doubt he may have also received some additional negative consequences when he got home.

Sex, Drugs, and Rock "n" Roll

Well, not anything to do with sex or music, but the title is catchy.

We have all heard the old saying, "What you don't know can't hurt you." In most cases, this is true. However, after what happened to my mother, she would beg to differ. She learned when you don't ask questions about what you don't know, it can end up causing you unnecessary pain and suffering. I will start with the end of the story and proceed backward.

It all began or ended, depending on how you look at it, with my dad yelling out from the porch to Mom. His exact words were, "Sabina, have you seen the hypodermic needle I keep in a box in this cupboard?" He was, of course, referring to the needle he used to inject gas or oil into various engines he was working with. That was when my mother lost it. Poor Dad did not see that one coming. Little did he know what had precipitated such a violent outburst from my mother. After the yelling and cursing subsided, and relief had washed over her, she was finally able to unleash tears of joy that had pent up inside of her for the last several days or weeks.

This was the time of the '60s. Free love, hippies, rock music, and psychedelic drugs were all in vogue. We three kids were in our teens, and while none of us was the typical "wild child," we sometimes did things our parents didn't always approve of. Of course, I am talking about myself and my youngest sister, Ruby. Wendy was the middle child who was always perfect and never caused our parents any grief. She consistently made the other two of us look bad. And to this day, she still DOES!! When she told our mom that she was going to a rock concert, of course, Mom completely trusted her and told her that would be great. However, she wasn't sure why anyone would want to look at a bunch of stones.

The event which triggered the angry outburst at my dad that I began this story with happened as follows. Mom was working in the porch, organizing and cleaning all the "stuff" accumulated over the winter. She found a small innocent-looking box during her cleaning, and when she opened it, she could not believe her eyes. Inside was a hypodermic needle, with the sharp, metal tip included. Even though there were no drugs in the box, this was a parent's worst nightmare.

The last thing she wanted was for Dad to find out one of their children was a "junkie." And since she was not sure, except for Wendy, which of the other two were into "shooting up," she decided to watch our every move to find the culprit. If only she would have known it couldn't have been me because I would have passed out before getting the needle anywhere close to my arm.

I don't specifically remember her checking our arms for track marks, but she did admit later she had done so pretending to check for something or other. Looking back on it, she was pretty sneaky because at no point did, we question what she was doing. I don't think she had hired any private investigators to follow us, but she was undoubtedly vigilant about where we went and with whom throughout that particular mystery.

For the short term, Mom did learn a valuable lesson. Her propensity for stubbornness did not keep her from getting herself into more predicaments in the future. For many years, this incident was recalled at family gatherings, and we all shared a good laugh at poor Mom's expense.

Curse You, Red Baron

During our younger years, we never had many pets. With our parents both working, they didn't feel it fair to leave an animal cooped up, alone, all day. I am sure we often pestered them about having a pet, so one time, they did relent and bought us some turtles. They were only a couple inches in diameter and spent their days in a small terrarium, eating and sleeping.

Turtles are not intelligent animals and try as I might, I could never teach them any tricks. I attempted to teach them to roll over, and nothing happened. They just sat there. When I placed them on their backs to get them to flip over, they would just lay there for hours with their feet wiggling up in the air. They couldn't even play "dead" right. We were not aware they secretly were Ninja Turtles, who were surprisingly good escape artists.

The sides of their enclosure were only a couple of inches tall, and somehow one of them managed to climb out. In the morning, when it was time to feed them, I noticed one of the inmates was missing and must have made a "run for the border." We immediately established a search party and set out to locate the missing reptile. We looked everywhere, and it was not to be found. Later on, as I was walking across a throw rug, I felt a crunch beneath my foot. FOUND IT!! Turtle soup, anyone?

It wasn't until our teen years that another pet entered our lives. Mom and Dad had traveled back to Saskatchewan to attend the funeral of one of our relatives. I was old enough, remember I never said mature enough, so that we three kids could stay home, alone. When our parents returned after the weekend, we couldn't believe what they had brought back with them. A friend at the funeral told them about the litter of puppies he had to give away, and that is how we came to own the world's smartest beagle. Being so very creative, we named him Snoopy. As it turned out, he was, indeed, quite the "flying ace."

This dog was brilliant, and he insisted on doing whatever it was we were doing. He had perfected the art of running away so we couldn't catch him and put him inside. That would allow him to follow you to wherever you were going. I told you in a previous post about his following me on my driver's test. This happened every time I would try to get in a vehicle and drive off. He would be waiting around the corner, and as soon as I thought the coast was clear, he was racing after me.

Of course, he was not the only one who I had to try to sneak away from. We had this little neighbour girl named Charmaine, who would patiently hide in the back of our truck box and wait for me to drive off. As soon as I was a couple of blocks away, she would pop up and beg to ride inside with me. Of course, being the compassionate person I am, I would relent and give her a little ride around town. After all, how could I resist such a cute little stalker? While I never actually let her ride in the cab with me, I will never forget the sight of her and Snoopy pointing their faces into the wind and enjoying the breeze rushing by.

Snoopy was the most spoiled dog the world has ever seen. He refused to eat dog food of any kind, wet or dry. He decided his "meal du jour" for every day of his life would be fried chicken livers. I am not sure how he discovered this passion, but he taught my mother well. She would fry up a batch of livers, which he would eat over the next several days. The biggest drawback to this delicacy was, over the years, he ended up putting on a pile of weight. In the end, he was pretty much approaching the shape of "round." He died a happy dog and never regretted his woefully unbalanced meals.

Before gaining a lot of weight, Snoopy was fast and very agile. One day, Dad and I were on the roof, replacing the shingles. While we were up there, we could hear Snoopy crying at the bottom of the ladder. I was busy applying tar to the bottom of the shingles when I happened to look over and see Snoopy's head coming above the roof. He had managed to climb the ladder and looked delighted with his fantastic accomplishment. Of course, I had to carry him down, but I was also pretty impressed at how he managed that trick.

One of Snoopy's favourite things to do was go camping. Each summer, we would all meet at "The Creek," a remote area not far from the Kikamun provincial park in BC. Our family, along with the Petersons, would spend hours camping, fishing, and sitting around campfires. Snoopy loved the freedom of being able to wander anywhere he wanted. There were moose, cougars, and even bears around, so Snoopy generally didn't stray too far from where we were camped.

Remember, I told you he was a sneaky dog who could track you without you even knowing it. One day, I was out on the creek, fishing, by myself. Maneuvering along the creek is often challenging, as there are willows everywhere, and with beavers around, you never know when you will step in a hole and sink up to your neck in water. While we had never actually seen a bear close to camp, the thought was always in the back of my mind.

It was while I was busy fishing that I suddenly heard a loud splashing sound behind me. I could tell something was running rapidly in my direction. I barely had time to take out my cleaning knife, which I am sure would be enough to stop a 700-pound bear. At the last second, the reeds parted and up popped Snoopy's head.

It was a sad day when it came time to say goodbye to our World War 1, Flying Ace. I often imagine him, in Doggie Heaven, snacking on some fried chicken livers, shouting out, "Curse you, Red Baron," as he flies his Sopwith Camel into the sunset.

A Perspective from Below

Does size really matter? Since I have spent my entire life coping with my physical disability of being vertically challenged, I would indisputably vote "yes." This is a disorder I share with many people. It's time we rally to try and end the blatant discrimination we face daily, throughout our entire lives. The problem is we are trapped in the middle. We are not big enough to qualify as average, so we are looked down upon by the regular folk. However, we do not qualify as "Little People" since we are too big by their standards. This is a real conundrum as we are mired in a "no man's" land.

Do any of you remember the 1977 song where Randy Newman sang about short people? A few of the lyrics state:

> Short people got no reason
> Short people got no reason
> Short people got no reason
> To live
>
> They got little hands
> And little eyes
> And they walk around
> Tellin' great big lies
> They got little noses
> And tiny little teeth

They wear platform shoes
On their nasty little feet

Can you imagine how embarrassing it was for me to be dancing while wearing my 6-inch platform shoes when the DJ would blast out that song?

The discrimination of the short starts at birth when the length of the baby is measured immediately after delivery. When the parents hear their baby is longer than the average of 50 cm, they can proclaim to the world that this is going to be a "tall" one. If the baby is less than 50 cm, they are not quite as enthusiastic, and you will hear the famous line that this one must have taken after the "short" side of the family.

The harassment of the short becomes much more pronounced once they reach school age. These days, people are quick to point out when they may be the recipient of profiling. This is defined as identifying an individual or group based on observed characteristics. I propose that profiling has been going on since the advent of cameras and class pictures.

In my case, it goes back to my kindergarten days. If you were to look at any one of my class pictures throughout my schooling, you would never have to look further than the front row to narrow down which student I was. Can you imagine the outrage and commotion that would result if the photographer lined up everyone, with the most attractive students sitting in front? Or what about if the subjects were lined up so those with the most extended noses were at the back because the extra distance would help make their proboscis look smaller? People would be outraged. Yet at every family gathering, you will hear the photographer shout out those famous words, "Short people in front."

It seems like height, or lack thereof, follows and haunts a person throughout their life. Imagine the embarrassment of going to Disneyland and waiting in a line, hoping to experience the thrill of spinning until you vomit. As you get closer to the front, there is a worker with a measuring stick in his hand. He uses this to determine if you are big enough to get on the ride. As you get closer, you are visually trying to determine if the bar on the stick will be low enough so when you try to walk under, it will hit you in the head.

As you get ready to be measured, you assume your ballet "Pointe" technique, where your entire mass is shifted upward onto the tips of your toes. As you struggle to stay tall and walk under the marker, you suddenly realize with horror that your head passes under, without touching, and you are not tall enough to ride. Insult is added to injury when your cousin, who is three years younger and has been blessed with the tallness gene, is allowed to continue onwards to enjoy the thrill of the ride. You get to go back and watch, with your mommy, as the others shout with glee as they are mercilessly tossed around until they are so dizzy, they can't stand.

One advantage for parents who have a child that is small for their age is it makes it easier to feed them. If the kid does not want to eat his beans, you tell them, "You have to eat your beans if you want to grow big." As I remember growing up, every food that tasted bad and that I could not stand eating was "good for me." If my parents didn't want me to eat something, I was informed it would stunt my growth. They went so far as to convince me that when the ice cream truck was playing music, it meant they were out of ice cream.

Most "normal-sized" people are unaware of the many restrictions shorter people are subjected to. For instance, when you are finally old enough to take your driver's test, are you aware that they can put certain conditions on your license? Of course, we are all familiar with Condition Code A, which means you must wear adequate lenses if your vision is not 20/20.

I bet many of you never heard of Condition Code B, which refers to "Special Circumstances." One of these conditions is you must use a cushion if you are not tall enough to see over the steering wheel. We can argue this makes safety sense. However, can you imagine having the rest of the students in your school know you can't drive without using a pillow? There is nothing a "dream date" finds sexier than when she snuggles over next to a guy in his car, only to discover he is propped up by a thick cushion.

I will be the first to admit that being short has often made me more determined and focused than I otherwise might have been. I have always felt I had to overcompensate at everything I did, to show people I could do whatever they could and maybe even more. However, if a short person tries too hard, he is criticized for that. We are accused of displaying a Napoleon Complex or Short Guy Syndrome.

We have all heard about some of the advantages of being short. The first relates to the fact that shorter people live longer than taller people. There are physiological reasons for this. Science has proven there is not as much stress on the heart in the pumping of blood through the circulatory system of someone who is shorter. Short people have faster reaction times and a heightened ability to accelerate body movements.

Short people are also less prone to the risk of cancer. The one benefit I had never heard of before is that being smaller puts you at a lower risk of heat exhaustion or sunstroke. This is either because tall people are closer to the sun, or short people are usually shaded by all the tall people around them.

I find it completely unacceptable that these days, there seems to be a medical procedure to fix almost every possible body scenario. Women can enhance or reduce parts of their bodies they are unhappy with. You can have your stomach stapled to help you lose weight. Your eyesight can be corrected with laser surgery. Billions of dollars are spent on various cosmetic surgeries, yet not one cent is being spent on ways to make you taller.

It was well known during the medieval ages that the "rack" was very effective at stretching people out and helping them gain a few inches. Just try to buy a good, economical rack, and you will quickly discover there are none to be found, not even on Amazon or eBay.

l would be remiss if I did not mention all the professional sports that are always on the lookout for smaller, less physically intimidating athletes. Oh wait, there is just one sport where these are suitable attributes, and we all know how many world-famous horse jockeys there are.

It is interesting to note I have now moved into a new category where my size is now secondary to my age. It does my heart good to hear tall people complain about how they are shrinking as they get older. When you are already short, you don't even notice the difference.

I am not sure if I have mellowed or resigned myself to my present condition of being old. It does not bother me as much as short jokes used to. I wear the badge of seniority with pride. It seems when you get old, you are almost expected to lose your filter and do or say things that previously would have been unacceptable. This is the get-out-of-jail-free card, and it is one I am planning on using to my full advantage for as long as I have left to live.

University

Please Pack
Your Knives and Go

This may come as a complete surprise to many people, but I am a closet *foodie*. I am hooked on watching cooking shows on television. It all started with *Iron Chef* and progressed to *Master Chef, Top Chef,* and when I am desperate, *Kid Chefs*. Lately, *Hell's Kitchen, Chopped,* and *Guy's Grocery Games* have been occupying my days. I am not sure what the fascination is since I don't even like to cook.

For me, sports have always been an integral part of my life. I have never encountered a sport I didn't like. Well, maybe curling, but I am just not old enough to appreciate the aesthetics of gliding down the ice without trying to bodycheck someone. While I may not have been great at any one sport, I can hold my own in a wide variety of sporting endeavors. When it comes to sports and pretty much life in general, I am uber-competitive. Sacrificing one's body to score or gain field position is a necessary evil of competition.

With cooking shows, I see people flying around in an enclosed space, occasionally knocking their competition to the ground if they are caught with their heads down. There is always the ever-present clock counting down the remaining seconds, never giving the participants enough time to fully reach their potentials. In the end, a victor is crowned, and the winners bask in the glory of having dominated their foe. Hold on. I just described a hockey game.

The similarities between these culinary shows and most sporting events are striking. There is usually a lot of blood, especially in cooking, where knives are their tools of the trade, along with sweat and tears. While some sports involve a group of judges, they tend to be very objective and do not openly criticize the contestants. Chefs judging others have no problem throwing the unsuccessful cooks to the gutter and voting them "off the island." I may be mixing up my metaphors with other reality shows, but it is a pretty accurate analogy.

Unfortunately, my love of watching cooking shows does not translate into an actual ability to cook. Granted, I can make a five-minute Kraft Dinner that will knock your socks off. However, my early cooking expertise was often limited to eating a hearty breakfast of leftover popcorn I had made the night before. Having grown up with a Ukrainian Baba for a mother, my role was to eat and eat and eat, not to cook. That was HER job.

I have often heard about newly married husbands who wish their new wives could cook like their mothers. This was not an issue for me. I am not saying my mother was not a good cook. I am saying she had her "limitations." She would whip up an incredible 12 course Ukrainian meal for 40 people every Christmas Eve. It was a masterpiece created by a true artist who could work magic. We never realized how talented she was until after she had passed, and we discovered it took five of us working together to accomplish what she had always done on her own.

Let's get back to Mom's limitations. I didn't realize until after I had left home that meat, especially steak, did not have to be black and shriveled to the size of a hockey puck to be "done." It was a good thing we had a dental plan because chewing on a piece of her steak always had the risk of breaking a tooth associated with it. It wasn't until my late teens that I discovered if you cooked a steak to medium or even, God forbid, rare, the meat did not taste like charred carbon.

My first adventures into the kitchen began when the time came for me to leave home and attend university in Lethbridge. Two friends and I rented an apartment together. The first thing we did was to establish the "ground rules" for living together. It was agreed that we would be on our own for breakfast and lunch. When it came to supper, we would take turns and whoever didn't cook was responsible for the dishes.

Some people use the terms supper and dinner interchangeably. I never realized the difference until I wrote this story. Supper is a typically light evening meal, while dinner is the main meal of the day and occurs at midday or in the evening. Therefore, I guess both can be correct.

Everything went perfectly for the first two days we lived together because I didn't have to cook until the third day. I had every intention of making a meal to remember, and I did not disappoint, but not in the way I was hoping. I decided upon a menu of a succulent roast of beef, mashed potatoes, and a side green salad.

On paper, this was a menu even Gordon Ramsey would be proud of. I avoided cremation of the roast by taking it out while there was still some juice left in it. The potatoes were boiled, just past the point of "al dente," and mashed to perfection. I chopped several tasty vegetable ingredients and composed a pretty impressive-looking salad.

Inspiration struck me, and apparently, it hit me in the head, way too hard. I decided if I were to add bacon on top of the potatoes and salad, I could be in the running for Top Chef. So, I cut up a pound of bacon into perfectly sized bits and fried it to perfection. And then my brain had an out-of-body experience. I carefully poured the bacon bits, grease and all, over the potatoes and salad. The result was a greasy, soggy pile of inedible mush.

Two good things happened next. First, we scrambled over to the A & W behind our apartment and ordered up our favourite Teen Burger plate. The second thing was I became the designated dishwasher, stripped of all future culinary responsibilities in the kitchen.

Isn't it interesting how one little mistake in life can change our futures? I am forever resigned to living vicariously through watching reruns of Bobby Flay.

If You Set the Bar
Low Enough

I learned many valuable things while going to university, but not many of them came from the classes I attended. Or, to be more precise, classes I did not participate in. It was my first year away from home, and I lived with two other friends in Lethbridge, in an apartment off-campus. It was the perfect location to live. We had an A & W outside our back fence, a KFC just across the other street, and we were five minutes from the "old" U of L campus. Most importantly, the Outrider Bar was only a five-minute drive down Mayor Magrath Avenue.

This was a transition year for the university, as they were just in the process of completing the "new" university buildings across the river on the West Side. As a result, I would have to take a bus downtown and transfer to another stop before traveling across the river for classes. I would catch a shuttle bus back to the old campus for all my lab work. I hope this daily marathon I was forced to endure helps explain why my class attendance was not necessarily exemplary. Of course, there were many other good reasons to skip classes.

The year was 1971, and there was a broad liberal shift sweeping across North America. This was the year the legal drinking age in Alberta dropped from 21 to 18. So here I was, going from the little town of Bow Island to the metropolis of Lethbridge, and on

September 12, two weeks after starting university, I was able to get into bars legally. You talk about timing being everything. Many of my older friends, who had been patiently waiting until they were 21, were pretty indignant that I was getting into the bars at the same time that they were.

In hindsight, I am confident this change in the legal age did nothing to help my academic progress. Coupled with the fact that one of my roommates was a bridge fanatic, it was no wonder that after staying up all night playing cards and drinking, I couldn't get up for classes.

My stay at the U of L, although only one year, still left many lasting impressions. I will not say I didn't pass any courses during my first year. However, while some students received letters from the Dean for their academic achievements, my letter emphatically stated that I might benefit more from taking the next year off to see if I was serious about post-secondary education.

In the Wink of an Eye

When one door closes, another opens. I applied to the University of Calgary. To my amazement, they accepted me, low grades and all. This time around, I was determined to learn from my mistakes. To avoid the temptation to skip classes, I would live right in the heart of the university and find accommodations in residence. There, I would learn through osmosis from all of the scholars surrounding me. I bet you are already guessing where this is heading.

I applied for residence and could not believe my good fortune when I learned I was assigned to an experimental trial floor. Even though we had gone through the sexual revolution of the 60s, there were still many prudish notions prevailing in our society. Never before in the institution's history had males and females cohabitated on the same floor.

We were the first floor in the university's history, where there were two wings of girls and one wing of guys, only separated by two solid steel doors leading into each wing. We didn't even have to take the stairs or elevators to access the promised land. I am pretty sure every guy on the floor, of which there were 34 of us, had visions of equally splitting our time amongst the 68 ladies who were yearning for male companionship.

It did not take long for reality to set in and for our fantasies to quickly fade into obscurity. The endless parties and debauchery never materialized, and it wasn't long before it felt more like living with a bunch of sisters. Since I was not into incest, I need to clarify that they were not all sisters. Along with five other guys that year, I met Mrs. Right on this floor and ended up getting married to her.

I met my wife, Irene, after she mercilessly murdered me in the common lounge area. Large groups of us would sit in a big circle facing each other. Cards were dealt out, with one of those cards being the Queen of Spades. This person was the "murderer." Hence, the game got its name of Murder. The game's object was to murder everyone else in the circle without getting caught. The murderer had to catch the eye of an unsuspecting victim and slay them by a wink of the eye. The object was for the murderer to slaughter as many victims as possible until someone spotted them winking.

I will never forget the night I noticed this gorgeous petite brunette sitting quietly across from me. We had never met before or even talked, but I had admired her from afar. I had found out through a friend that her name was Irene. She looked so INNOCENT. Well, it was about three hands into the game when she massacred me. I have never seen anyone who could wink as quickly and subtly as this brown-eyed beauty, who finished me off in a heartbeat. I was killed so quickly that I didn't even have time to protest.

This was the beginning of the end, or should I say the beginning of the beginning. We ended up taking many a long walk together around the university campus. I remember holding her close as we talked and the snow gently falling on us. Not only had she murdered me, but she had shown me I could not live without her.

So, there you have it. This year will mark our 47th anniversary. I would be lying if I told you that it has been all laughter, wine, and roses. I did start to get a little nervous on day 11 of our self-isolation during the pandemic. I am very supportive that she has begun crocheting again to help fill the time. I did become a little concerned when I looked in the pattern book she was using, and discovered that she was working on something that resembled a noose.

Walk of Shame

We have all heard that you don't get a second chance to make a good first impression. If your first impression is very good or very bad, it can stay with you for a very long time. As I indicated earlier, when I moved to Calgary to attend university, I decided to live in the student dormitories. It was during this first night in residence that my opportunity to make a big impression occurred.

I did not leave for Calgary until after I finished work in Bow Island. By the time I checked in at the registration desk and found my room, it was late. Most of the people who lived on the floor had gone out drinking by that time, so I did not have the opportunity to meet anyone. My roommate had not yet arrived, so I was alone in my room.

I went to bed early, and when I woke up at about 3:00 am, I needed to go to the bathroom. I lived at the end of the wing, and the bathrooms were at the other end, down the hall. I figured since there was no one else around, I would just walk down in my underwear. As I exited from my room, I left the door, so the latch rested gently against the stop. The doors had an automatic lock when they closed, so I ensured it was not shut completely.

I proceeded to walk to the end of the hall. When I pushed the door open to the bathroom, I felt a slight breeze which must have created a vacuum, resulting in a click that I heard at the other end of the hall. My worst fears materialized when I realized that click was *my* door locking shut. There I was, dressed only in underwear, locked out of my room. Talk about your "Walk of Shame." After knocking on a couple of doors and being told to do some physically impossible things, I finally found the Floor Senior who had a master key and solved my dilemma. No one could ever accuse me of not making a lasting first impression.

Rub-a-Dub-Dub;
Someone's Going in the Tub

Believe it or not, university residence life was not "all work and no play." I have no idea if any of the activities we used to engage in are still occurring. I guess with all the political correctness and thin skins which abound these days, boredom reigns supreme. For those who would discredit such childish behaviours, many of us did grow up to become productive members of society. Heck, some even became teachers, principals, and superintendents.

The most popular activity everyone eventually participated in, although not always willingly, was the art of Tubbing. This was pretty much like it sounds. Someone would fill one of the bathtubs 3/4 full of cold water. To ensure it was shocking enough, you would add ice cubes to enhance the effect. Now for the fun part. A group of us would decide in advance who the "victim" was, but it had to be a surprise attack. We would knock on the door of the unsuspecting target, and when he or she opened it, it was game over for them.

The struggling and usually screaming individual would be carried slowly towards the ice-filled tub. They immediately knew what was happening, and the anticipation was vital to ensure the captor's maximum amount of anxiety. They were ceremoniously held over the ice-filled tub, just waiting for what was to come. Once the target realized the futility of the fight, the body was quickly and unceremoniously immersed below the surface of the water. There were strict rules about this. We didn't want to drown anyone, but no one ever stopped to think about heart failure. To my knowledge, the only casualties were hairdos and shrinkage.

As I said, everyone received at least one tubbing throughout the year. Everyone, except Andy! To put this in perspective, Andy was approximately 6 feet 4 inches tall and weighed 250 pounds. It was not that we didn't try to tub Andy, but even if we could have managed to carry him to the tub, there is no way he would have fit in. In a situation such as this, it was necessary to invoke our creative juices.

Andy received special treatment. We managed to tie him to a chair with a fellow student's mountain climbing rope. Once he was securely fastened to the chair, we could carry him to the shower, where we set him inside and blasted the cold water onto him. Of course, a few people did have buckets of ice water to help emulate the effect of tubbing. It was a good thing Andy was a gentle giant, but I can assure you that many of us kept our distance for several days after.

Water, Water, Everywhere

Another one of our water sports involved the concept of torpedoing other floors. There were large garbage receptacles in the lobby and bathrooms. These cans held around 5 gallons of water. We would summon the elevator to our floor and carefully choose which of the other floors would be "torpedoed." We would push the light for that particular floor, take the can filled with water, set it inside the elevator, and lean it back against the doors as they closed. There was a definite learning curve to doing this, which resulted in the elevator often getting drenched. When the elevator reached the floor that had been chosen, the unsuspecting travelers waiting to get in would be greeted by a gush of water flooding the floor of their lobby.

As you can imagine, no good deed goes unpunished. This usually resulted in a battle royale. All the students from that floor, armed with small water-filled buckets and water balloons, would invade the floor that they believed started the battle. The guys, who were not as conscientious about maintaining proper decorum, would often shed down to their boxers or briefs to avoid getting their clothes drenched.

It was during the heat of battle when one of the residents, clad only in their "tighty whities," ran to the bathroom to fill his bucket. When he ripped open the door to join the fray, he was greeted by his parents, who had come for a surprise visit. I am sure they were delighted with how their monetary investment in his education was paying off.

There was one other popular water game, but it was only played during frigid weather. This involved a group of people gaining access to the room of their prey. Various items of the victim's clothing and bedding would be soaked in a tub. Once the outside window was opened, the drenched items would be pasted to the outside wall of the building, where they immediately froze in place.

When it was 40 below zero, the clothing froze solid immediately. It used to be hilarious, walking home from class and looking up to see several items frozen stiff outside someone's room. I can personally remember coming back from writing a test and looking up to see just such a scenario. I began to laugh and count at the same time. As soon as I noticed the room was on the fifth floor, two down from the end, I realized it was MY room. Do you have any idea how difficult it is to fit frozen sheets through a small window?

Misdirected Divine Inspiration

People never ask me how I get my ideas for stories, but I will tell you anyhow. The best way to describe it is that it is a "gift." Some gifts are valuable, and others are worthless. Most would agree my talent lies in the latter category. We all know everyone is good at something and the goal in life is to discover what that something is. The only thing worse than never discovering your gift is to find out that your gift is as useful as the "g in lasagna."

It all started way back in university. I was a science major, so most of my classes involved lab work and write-ups reporting on the scientific investigations we were experimenting with. Unfortunately, I had to take some coursework outside of my major. I quickly discovered that the humanities professors felt they could better evaluate their students by assigning papers to write. Did they not realize that these damn literary manifestos cut severely into our social lives? In my case, this amounted to one entire night per paper.

You need to remember that back in the 70s, electricity was not yet invented; Oops, I mean computers. The only option we had to cursive diction was to plunk away on a manual typewriter. While White Out was available as an editing option, I did not have the patience or time to wait for it to dry. As a result, whatever keys I struck resulted in words and sentences and ended up in the finished copy. Being a self-acclaimed procrastinator, I would always wait until the night before to start my paper and stay up all night to complete it. I usually ended up finishing minutes before I had to rush off and slide it under the professor's office door.

Before you call me names such as lazy, indolent, slothful, lethargic, languorous, or torpid, I must explain that I am in some very famous company here. I am sure many of you have heard of a somewhat obscure band called *The Beatles* and their lead singer, Paul McCartney. What you may not know is that one of the highest-grossing songs of all time, *Yesterday*, was composed by Paul, from start to finish, in 10 minutes. He had a vivid dream, and as soon as he awoke, he wrote done the melody and lyrics, and *Yesterday* was born.

Another example is the song *American Woman*, written by a Canadian band called *The Guess Who*. This song was the product of a jam session at a curling rink in Ontario. When lead guitarist, Randy Bachman, broke a string, he replaced it and started playing a circular guitar riff during the tuning process. When the rest of the band joined in, the lead singer Burton Cummings made up words on the spot, and the rest is history.

Luckily, someone in the crowd had a cassette recorder, and the band borrowed it to help recreate the song. A little-known fact is that what was going through Burton's mind during the piece was that American women seemed to get older quicker than Canadian girls. This made them more dangerous, and when he said, "American Woman, stay away from me," he was worried that those older women would steal his innocence.

In reality, the only difference between these famous songwriters and me is that their final product was gold. I also have made money from my writing. I used to have a roommate in university who was basically illiterate. I would write his papers for him, and he would reimburse me with a case of beer for my efforts. No doubt I got the better deal there, but he always seemed happy with the C- grade I was usually able to obtain for him.

Using a sports expression, I would categorize my writing talents as that which happens when "You are in the zone." Admittedly, most times, it is more like the Twilight Zone because I have no idea where some of the bizarre ideas come from.

It is true that when I sit down at my computer to write, something takes over, and I suddenly find myself in an "out of body experience." A force seems to take control of my fingers, and they begin to glide across the keyboard. Often it looks something like this:

Asdfkwjeijfwkl;efklskljdfeskjowpjeiorjwoejwoiejiojaiojewri oewjiorjioewjriojewijroiewjrijweoirjwoiejriwejrisdkdldfkg;lkdf gkdfpokpodgkdpfokgpodfksgokdsofkgpodfkgpokdfpogkdspof kgpodfkgpodfkgpokdfpogkdpofkgpodfkgpokdpogkg

Other times, actual words and paragraphs amazingly appear on the page. The thing that generally surprises me the most is that out of nowhere, a "50-cent word" will come to mind. I am not sure if you have ever heard of a 50-cent word. This describes a term that is usually over eight letters in length, sounds very intelligent, and most people would never think of using it in their daily conversations.

Most of the time, I have no clue whether the word is being used correctly in a grammatical sense, if it is the correct tense, or even spelled right. Heck, most times, I have no clue if I am even using the correct definition. I have never let a small detail like incorrect usage stop me. I proudly place the word somewhere in the text, hoping no one else will notice if it is wrong. Usually, I find people are too embarrassed to admit they don't know the meaning of the word so that I can generally get away with it.

One of my greatest strengths, or maybe my greatest weakness, is that I am a perfectionist. Not that I create perfection, but I am *never* satisfied with my final product. It was so much simpler in the old days when I would accept my C grade and wait until the night before my next paper was due to start the process all over again.

Where Were You When...

Everyone can relate to specific memorable events that occurred in their past. They will tell you that they can remember exactly where they were and what they were doing during a specific incident. For me, there are some events that I can visualize in great detail as to when they happened and where I was. For some others, it is a distant memory, where the surrounding details have faded.

The earliest major event I can remember occurred on November 22, 1963. I had to look up the date, but I remember exactly where I was and what I was doing. I was ten years old and just recovering from a bout of "measles." Since I was still contagious, I was quarantined at home and spent the day watching television. I remember I was in the middle of watching some Western movie when all of a sudden, it was interrupted by a "News Flash."

The announcer was almost crying, and he kept repeating that there had been a tragedy in Dallas, Texas. The President of the United States, John Fitzgerald Kennedy, had been shot while riding in a parade. While the significance of this event was lost on me as a 10-year-old, I will never forget that I never did get to see the end of that movie I had been watching.

Another event that occurred around the same time was not nearly as earth-shattering, although it was pretty significant for a little town like Grassy Lake. My friend's parents owned the Esso Service Station, and we would often play in and around the area. One day, a black limousine pulled up to the gas pumps. Out stepped several people, dressed in suits.

I knew they must have been pretty important because it wasn't long before many adults from inside the restaurant came out to meet with one gentleman, in particular. I remember him shaking my hand, but it wasn't until later that I found out who it was. The gentleman who took the time to shake hands and say hello was none other than John Diefenbaker, the 13th Prime Minister of Canada from 1957-1963.

It seems that celebrities' deaths are some of the most noteworthy news items of the day. I can remember August 16, 1977, vividly, as I was sitting in a Barber's chair getting my hair cut in downtown Calgary. The radio was on when the music was interrupted to tell of Elvis Aaron Presley's death. He had died from a heart attack. This may have resulted from too many peanut butter and banana sandwiches. Although I was not a total Elvis fanatic, he was an icon who changed the face of music forever, and his songs and memories live on to this very day.

Two very significant deaths occurred within days of my birthday, and even now, when I celebrate my birthday, I am reminded of these celebrities. On August 31, 1997, Princess Diana died as a result of a tragic car accident. Her funeral was on September 6, which is my actual birth date. On September 5, one day before Princess Di's funeral, Mother Teresa passed away at 87 years of age. She was a Catholic Missionary who spent her entire life helping the poor in Calcutta, India. Nineteen years after her death, she was canonized as a Saint. That week, in 1997, the world lost two amazing women.

No one will ever forget the events surrounding one of the most tragic days in American history, which occurred on September 11, 2001. I lived in Foremost and worked as the Deputy Superintendent with the Prairie Rose School Division, out of Dunmore. I remember getting in my car to leave for work and turning on the radio to discover a plane had hit one of the Twin Towers in New York

City. There was a great deal of chaos and confusion, and announcers could not believe how such an accident could happen.

It was not long after that another plane struck the second tower, and by then, it was becoming clear that there was nothing acciden-tal about these circumstances. I remember getting to the office and everyone sitting around watching the television monitor and won-dering what was in store for the future in terms of global peace.

Bursting with Pride

Of all events I remember from my past, the one that left the most significant impact occurred in September of 1972. I was on my way to a 10:00 am class in the Science Theatres at the University of Calgary. When I entered the main foyer, there were hundreds of students standing around, ready to watch Game eight of the 1972 Canada/USSR Summit series.

I had a decision to make. I am sure you will be shocked to hear that I didn't make it to the class that morning. I ended up watching an historic hockey game that may never be surpassed as far as excitement and the promotion of national unity. I will attempt to provide the background that led to this monumental event.

In the Olympics, the USSR(Russia) had dominated the sport of ice hockey for years, winning the majority of gold medals. Canada and the US were never able to send their best players because the Olympics did not allow professionals to compete.

Before the Olympics in 1972, there was talk that the rules would change to accommodate professional hockey players. When this deal fell through, Canada and the USSR decided to play a series amongst themselves, pitting Canada's professional best against the Olympic team of the USSR. This was named the Summit Series and occurred during September of 1972, with four games being played in Canada, followed by four games in the USSR.

Before the series, Canada sent two ambassadors over to the USSR to scout the strengths and weaknesses of the USSR team. They spent just four days and reported that the USSR team was nothing more than a ragtag squad of outclassed amateurs. They believed that a little-known 20-year old goalie named Vladislav Tretiak was the weakest link on the team.

They had watched just one game, and apparently, this was the day after Tretiak had partied too hard because of his upcoming marriage. Goaltending legend Jacques Plante felt so sorry for Tretiak that he went to the Soviet dressing room with an interpreter before the first game in Canada. His goal was to brief the Soviet goalie on the Canadian players' shooting tendencies so that he wouldn't be too severely embarrassed.

There was no doubt in the minds of any Canadian fans or hockey players about the outcome of this series. It was predicted to be an eight-game romp in the park, with the Canadians easily winning all eight games.

When the Canadians lost the first game 7-3, everyone was stunned as the young Goalie, Tretiak, robbed the Canadians blind. When the Canadians came back to win 4-1 in game two, the order had been restored to the Universe. Game three ended up as a 4-4 tie. They did not play overtime. When the Russians won the 4th game by a score of 5-3, the Canadian fans loudly booed the team, and Captain Phil Esposito made his famous speech berating the fans for not supporting their efforts.

Heading back to Russia, the Canadians began to think the impossible thought, that perhaps, they could lose this series. When the Russians came back and scored four unanswered goals to win 5-4 in the fifth game, the reality was that Canada had to win the last three games to take the series. The next two games were won by Canada by scores of 3-2 and 5-4, setting up the eighth game with a winner take all prize. The game was tied at 5-5, with less than a minute left. The

Russian announcers claimed victory as their team had scored more goals overall so that a tie would give the series title to their team.

With 34 seconds left in the game, Paul Henderson scored the goal heard around the world, giving Canada the series win. When the final buzzer sounded, everyone in the building, where we were standing, was cheering and yelling at the top of their lungs. When they played the national anthem, every student sang *O Canada* at the top of their lungs. There were more tears, and national pride exhibited at that moment than I have ever felt any time since. For a brief period, all of Canada was united, and we showed fierce pride in what we had accomplished.

What a difference from today, where the government seems to be more concerned with dividing the country up and pitting us against each other. If I were to suggest "Divide and Separate," would that sound too much like a bra commercial? Maybe, there is such a thing as the "Good Ole Days."

Yes Master

As I mentioned previously, my life was never carefully planned out in advance. It seemed that whenever something needed to happen to me, there was some outside force that made it possible.

While going through the motions attending university, I learned many things. These included playing bridge and staying up all night playing road race games. The result was that it often involved my missing class and even missing assignments and tests. As a result, I failed my first year at the University of Lethbridge. I was fortunate enough to get accepted into the University of Calgary, and that is where I continued my busy social life.

It wasn't until I met my wife, Irene, that I decided unless I won the lottery and could spend the rest of my life attending university, I had to get my act together. And snap me into shape, she did. There is not a doubt in my mind that without her guidance and support, I would not have completed my second year of post-secondary education.

It became clear, having already wasted a year, that I was not prepared to spend another six years working to become a pharmacist. With many family members in the field of education, I decided teaching would be a better career choice. I was very intrigued by the idea of having two months "off" in the summer. Little did I understand how hard you had to work for the other ten months.

I taught junior high science in Calgary for the next six years. I was very fortunate to work with many excellent teachers who had aspirations of bettering themselves. When a group of them decided they would pursue further education, I thought I would go along for the ride. At the time, several institutes from the United States were interested in providing coursework that would earn us a Masters of Education degree.

Gonzaga University, located in Spokane, Washington, agreed to fly their professors to Calgary to instruct our cohort group of 15 future administrators. On Friday afternoon, as soon as classes ended, we all drove to a school in downtown Calgary where at 5:00 pm, we would spend the next four hours as students. The next day, we met again and spent eight hours learning how to be administrators.

We were given assignments that had to be completed for the following weekend. We did this just about every weekend for the next two years. While it was a lot more work than I had anticipated, we could complete the coursework without having to quit our day jobs for two years. The years flew by, and soon it was time for the program's last segment. We had to spend July and August of the final year in Spokane, attending classes at Gonzaga.

Typically, a Master's degree requires you to write a dissertation and defend it in front of a group of experts from the university. When the big day arrived, it turned out to be not quite as rigorous as we had feared. We had to book a reservation at the campus restaurant, where we met with two professors. Over breakfast, they asked questions about my dissertation, which related to the importance of athletics in developing a well-rounded student. Whether or not I passed depended on one major component. I was required to pay for all three breakfasts. Talk about a deal I couldn't pass up.

Several years later, some of these same colleagues who had organized the Master's program decided it might be a good idea to get a Doctorate. While I had the necessary unreadable handwriting to qualify as a doctor, the last thing I wanted to do was go through another two years of hard work. I could never get used to being called Doctor Leffler. And besides, what kind of doctor faints at the sight of blood.

Marriage and Family

A Sign from Above

You always hear people say things like "Karma is a b$&ch" and "What goes around, comes around." That may indeed be cosmically possible. Sometimes if you live long enough, an event occurs which triggers a memory. Your mind makes a connection, indicating you "deserved" it. Then again, maybe karma is for real, as all my wannabe Buddhist friends keep telling me.

The 1960s were an era of western movies, *The Lone Ranger*, and all things cowboy. A must-have for all kids was a realistic looking toy gun. We lived for Saturday Night when Gunsmoke came on the television. Marshal Dillon, played by James Arness, would weekly be involved in a shootout and run all the bad guys out of Dodge. I will never forget the Christmas I received a Marshal Dillon Holster and two metal six-shooters, not those cheap plastic ones produced today.

The essential prop was the plastic marshal badge that could be pinned proudly to your chest. To make things more realistic, these guns were designed to fire small explosives called "caps." When fired, it would make a pretty impressive bang, and we felt like we were firing actual bullets. It was always exciting when my friend Erin and I would line up back to back and slowly take ten steps away from each other. When we spun around, I would have my six-shooters drawn and ready to fire before Erin knew what hit. I was the fastest six shooting, slammin' gunslinger in the west.

The next phase in most kid's western evolution was the progression to a long rifle "bb gun." The entire town was our hunting grounds. No one ever told us you couldn't shoot guns in town. A large field by the school had many gophers that made perfect targets. No one complained about getting rid of the pests that made all the holes that kids could trip in.

Another target that required a little more skill was the birds. I wish I could say we never shot any of the "good" birds, but unfortunately, at that age, anything with wings was game. However, there was a real downside with shooting into the trees because sometimes, if we missed the bird, we didn't miss the neighbour's window.

We have all heard of cross-training where you do a couple of different sports together. I may have been the first to invent cross hunting. We always seemed to have hundreds of seagulls who loved nothing more than to scrounge for food in the garbage. Our bb guns didn't seem to be powerful enough to take down a seagull. I came up with a different plan.

My dad used to take me fishing, so I decided to bait my hook with some bread and cast it towards the garbage can. It didn't take long, and all of a sudden, I had hooked a seagull. There I was, watching a seagull fly around like a kite. For a few minutes, it was exciting to watch the bird dip and soar, trying to get away. Then, it hit me. How was I going to get the bird off the line?

I ended up having to reel it in and kill it to get the hook out. This was not the making of a serial killer, as I can remember feeling horrible about what I had done, and that was the last time I fished out of the water.

It wasn't until years later, when I was a young adult, that I decided maybe I would try my hand at big game hunting. I wasn't ready for a deer or a bear, but I had heard pheasant was a tasty bird. I went out with my friend, Dick, who was a hunter. He had an extra shotgun that he let me use. I had never taken a hunter safety program. I was more of a risk to my friend than I was to any birds we might encounter.

I can remember walking down a field trying to chase up a pheasant. I was not ready because sometimes you almost have to step on them to get them to fly away. When the bird took off, literally a couple of feet away from me, I was so surprised that by the time I could raise the gun to shoot, the bird was long gone.

Getting skunked by the pheasants, we decided to alter our plans and try something where we might have a better chance of actually being successful. There were no pear trees, but there were lots of partridges. My partner was playing a hunting dog's role, walking along the tree line in hopes of scaring out some prey. When he disturbed a flock of partridges, they came flying towards me. All I remember is pointing my gun towards the sky and pulling the trigger.

The next thing I see is one of the birds falling like a rock from the sky. When it hit the ground, it wasn't dead, and its body began to flop around. I yelled at my partner and asked him what to do. When he told me to step on its head and kill it, there was not a chance that was happening. That was the end of my hunting career.

Flash forward to the summer of 1974. It was early August, and just a few days before, Irene and I were getting married. The wedding was to be held in Bow Island, with the reception at the Grassy Lake Hall. The best men and I had rented our tuxedos from a store located in downtown Calgary. The day I was to pick the penguin suits up was overcast with some drizzling rain. I had parked in a parkade and had to walk a few blocks to the store.

I can remember walking along the street and passing under many awnings on the way to my destination. As I stated earlier, it was drizzling, so when I was not under an awning, I could feel the rain coming down from above. I faintly remember one splash landing on my head, but I didn't think anything of it. I continued to the store and met with a nice young lady who helped me out and gave me the tuxedos to take with me. I don't remember her looking at me funny or acting strange.

As I was walking back to my car, I remember reaching up to scratch my head. A few seconds later, I used the same hand to scratch my nose. It was then that it hit me. What was that horrible smell? I looked around, but there was nothing I could see lying dead on the street. As my finger again passed close to my nostrils, the stench of ammonia permeated my olfactory lobes. Whatever it was, it smelt like "S#*T."

It wasn't until I got into my car and looked in the rear-view mirror that I saw "it." There, on top of my head, for all the world to see, was a white and green gob of bird crap. I was mortified as I replayed the last 20 minutes in my head. I had walked by many people on my way to the store. I had spent 10 minutes talking to the girl who had helped me with the tuxedos. Wouldn't you think someone would have said something about the droppings on my head? Karma maybe, but what happened later, most definitely.

The next time karma visited me was at a slow-pitch tournament in Coaldale. We had finished the game and were celebrating on the patio of a bar. I had just ordered a beer and hamburger. The waitress set it down, and just as I was going to reach for it to put on some condiments, a seagull flew over and did the job for me. It deposited a load of white, smelly excrement all over the burger and halfway up my arm. I am thinking the seagull probably had a great-great-grandfather who I had met when I was a young boy who couldn't afford a kite and decided to go fishing for seagulls.

Points; Easy Come, Easy Go

It seems everywhere you look these days, stores, credit card companies, hotels, airlines, everyone is offering some type of points plan. Loyalty points can be redeemed for hotel stays, airline flights, free movies, gas, or even cold, hard cash. The idea is that you tend to frequent only one competitor resulting in you spending all of your money in one place, rather than spreading it around.

Some of these plans require yearly membership fees, while others are free. The program I am going to highlight requires a lifetime subscription. Not only does this plan require complete and total loyalty, but any outside purchases result in dire consequences. This plan is the oldest currency known to mankind. For all the single gents out there, it is a topic every bit as foreign as "Bitcoin."

I am, of course, talking about "husband points." These points take months to earn. While some plans have expiration dates and shelf lives, the points a husband can earn can completely disappear in one fell swoop. Depending on the severity of your transgression, you can even end up in a deficit situation. All married men are under the impression that there are actual rewards at the end of the rainbow. However, there are no known cases of any married man who has ever lived long enough to redeem said points.

There are many ways points may be accrued. Chores around the house are one of the most basic methods possible. Compliments, the purchase of flowers and jewelry, and making breakfast in bed are also areas that may result in small or large numbers of points. The ironic thing is that the accumulated points are never actually kept on record anywhere. No one but the wife knows exactly how many points have been earned. Just like a flash flood or earthquake, everything can be lost and destroyed through one innocent or accidental event.

I will give you an example from personal experience. It occurred one night while we were sitting around the supper table. My wife and I, along with our two daughters and son, were eating supper together. Family meals are a lost art that has gradually made a comeback a la the Coronavirus quarantine. Our daughters, Andrea and Courtney, never had a problem sharing and would go into great detail to describe their entire day from the time they woke up. Our son, Dustin, however, was a man of few words. With two sisters, when did he ever get a chance to speak?

During our meal, a brief moment occurred where both girls had to stop talking to take a breath. When Dusty started to speak, everyone was shocked and immediately stopped what they were doing to listen to him. He spoke quietly, yet his manner indicated he had something important to tell us. He described how at school that day, acting roles were assigned, and he was chosen for one of the parts.

I immediately jumped in with some positive reinforcement and told him how proud I was of him. I asked him what role he was going to assume. He proudly indicated he would be playing the part of a middle-aged man who had been married for 25 years. "Just like you, Dad," he stated. At that moment, my brain stopped working, and my tongue took on a life of its own. Without even considering the consequences of what I was about to say, I heard my voice blurt out, "That's okay, son, maybe you'll get a speaking part next year."

I have to tell you, up until that moment, I had been on a streak. Everything had been going better than I could have hoped for, and it seemed, over the weeks, I had finally earned enough points that I was very close to finding out what the elusive holy grail of husband points could earn me. Well, without a sound, all it took was just one look from my wife, and I knew not only had my "points" been flushed down the toilet, but I could look forward to at least one night on the sofa.

No Room at the Inn

Irene and I were married on August 3, 1974. I was still going to university, and Irene was the breadwinner. She served as a teacher assistant in the French department, first at Bishop Carol High School and then Mount Royal College. We were the typical struggling newlyweds, and the last thing we could afford was a trip somewhere exotic.

I had a summer job working for New West Homes, and I was only able to get a few days off. We had talked about possibly driving to Penticton to spend a few days on the beach of Skaha Lake. The only firm plan I made was to reserve the night of our wedding at the Heritage Inn in Taber. Being a typical guy, I didn't think past the wedding night.

The next day, over breakfast, we decided we were not in the mood for a long drive to British Columbia. We agreed that the two hours it would take to drive to Waterton would be time well spent. Unfortunately, I didn't realize Waterton can be very busy in the summer. You cannot just expect to drive up to a hotel and be guaranteed a room.

When we arrived at the Bayshore Inn in Waterton, we received a similar response that Joseph and Mary had received many years earlier when they visited Bethlehem during the Roman census. We were informed there were no rooms at the Inn or anywhere else in the whole town.

We ended up having to drive a half-hour to Pincher Creek, where we stayed in a beautiful 1-star hotel. It had lovely bluebirds painted on the outside, so I figured it looked kind of "honeymooney"; Irene, not so much. Fortunately for me, we did manage to get a room in Waterton for the next few days, and we ended up having a delightful stay. Not that I remember us actually seeing too many of the sights.

Promise Less, Deliver More

My ex-girlfriend and I celebrated our 25th Wedding Anniversary on August 3, 1999. Irene does not appreciate me calling her this, but once we were married, she did become my ex. Who, in their wildest dreams, could have believed Irene would put up with me for that long? I often tell her I am convinced that the only reason she married me is to be guaranteed a spot in Heaven. Only an angel could resist the temptation to kill me on a daily basis.

Knowing how much she has done for our family, I decided to make our Silver Anniversary one anniversary that neither of us would ever forget. That is precisely what happened, just not in the way I had hoped.

I have always believed in business, life, and most especially marriage, that the secret to success is to "promise less and deliver more." Even though it is very tempting to want to play the politician and promise the "moon," usually all that does is set you up for a one-way trip to the doghouse. Therefore, when I purchase something, I believe it is my right to expect, nay demand, EVERYTHING an ad or salesperson has promised. Nothing more and certainly nothing less.

Since we had met in Calgary and spent the first eight years of our married life there, I decided Calgary should be the spot to celebrate the "BIG 25". Over the years, I had often visited the Delta Bow Valley Inn and was always impressed by their professionalism and attention to detail. The location was perfect, as it was downtown and close to many fine restaurants. When I contacted the Inn regarding any special packages or promotions they offered, my interest was immediately piqued when they mentioned the Honeymoon Suite Adventure.

I ended up reserving the Honeymoon Suite, which featured an in-room jacuzzi tub. Does it get any more romantic than that? I also decided to spare no expense and upgraded to the "Romance Package." I was quoted the rate of $309 + taxes. At the time, that was more than three times the price of a standard room, so I was giddy with the prospects of the romantic adventure in our future.

We arrived at 4:00 p.m. on August 3, 1999, which was the pre-arranged time of arrival. Upon checking in, I was told our reservation in the honeymoon suite was all set and all we had to do was enjoy ourselves. The receptionist was most friendly, and we immediately felt welcome. When I asked about parking, I was given a pass and told I could park anywhere in the parkade. I had not copied down everything included in the package, so I had no idea that valet parking was included. I found out at the end of our stay that I should have asked for this.

When we got to the room, I carried Irene across the threshold. Actually, I had her jump up on my back because my arms were carrying the luggage. The first impression of the room did not disappoint. It was exactly as I had hoped it would be. We decided to settle in for a nice jacuzzi soak before supper. When I looked in the closet for the thick, luxurious bathrobes that were supposed to be part of the package, there was only one in the room. I suggested we use "rock, paper, scissors" to decide who got the robe, but Irene wasn't impressed with that idea.

I remember reading the sign prominently displayed in the bathroom. It stated that the hotel was so confident in their staff that if anything were missing, the guests would be guaranteed the first night free. I believe it was called the Blue-Ribbon guarantee. I was a little disappointed when I had to phone down to the desk to request an additional robe. The robe finally arrived, just as we were leaving the room to go out for supper.

I had made reservations at a new and trendy restaurant not far from our hotel. When we got there, I quickly discovered I might have inadvertently committed another mistake. Irene's culinary tastes tend to lean closer to the more traditional fare. When we looked at the menu and the items featured, moose, caribou, elk, and various other critters, I could tell by the look on her face that she would have preferred McDonald's. I apologized profusely to the maître de, and we decided to try another restaurant. We were not far from the legendary Hy's steakhouse. In the past, we had been treated to several excellent meals there, so our hopes were once again renewed.

Fortunately, we were able to get in without a reservation, and we settled into a pre-meal drink to begin an evening of romance. We both ordered the steak and lobster and could not wait, as we were running a little later than expected and we were both starved.

When the meal came, we both started to dig in. The steak was perfect, but when we tried to dip the lobster in the melted butter, the butter was stone cold and barely in a liquid state. We finally got our waiter's attention and sent the butter back to be reheated. It seemed like a simple request. After 10 minutes, I asked him to check on it. When he brought them back, they were still cold. We immediately sent it back again, and I offered to put them in a microwave myself if they were too busy.

By the time we got the butter back, it was indeed hot, but everything else was cold. Any other time, I may have chalked it up to bad luck, but I was so intent on making the night perfect that I was starting to get extremely annoyed. We finished up our cold meals and left with the reassurance that the evening could still be saved by what was coming next.

As part of our package, I had previously arranged for the champagne and strawberries to be delivered to the room at 8:30 p.m. We arrived back at the room at 9:00 p.m., and there was nothing there.

Not wanting to spoil the surprise, I suggested we go to the Calgary Tower for a view of the lights. We did this and came back to the room at about 10:30 p.m. I was sure everything would be there by then.

The Comedy of Errors Continues

When we got back to the room, I was most disappointed to see nothing had been delivered. By now, I was losing patience, but I still stayed polite. When I informed the girl at the desk, she looked at the computer, and it indeed did say that everything was to be delivered by 8:30. She was most apologetic and called the manager. He was also most concerned and promised everything would be dispatched immediately. He suggested that he send up a bottle of Dom Perignon Champagne to make up for the earlier mistakes. I was not that impressed with his gesture because I knew my wife was up in the room, wondering what I was doing.

In an attempt to avoid disappointment in the morning, I also asked if breakfast was included in the package. By now, I was not taking anything for granted. The manager commented that we should have received a $25 gift certificate in the welcome basket. I informed him that there was no welcome basket. Once again, I felt that if I didn't ask or beg for the things, I wasn't going to get them.

I went back to the room, and within five minutes, the champagne and strawberries arrived. Included also was the breakfast certificate. Unfortunately, it was not the surprise I had intended since I had to explain to Irene what was happening. It only took another

30 minutes for me to calm down before we spent the rest of a very romantic evening.

The following day, we had a delicious breakfast in the room. It was delivered promptly and was excellent. We decided to have one final hot tub. While we were in the tub, the phone rang. The person who brought the breakfast forgot to extinguish the flame on the cart and asked if we could put the burner out. He offered to come up and do it, but we did not want to be interrupted. It was not a big deal to extinguish the flame. Combined with everything else, it would have almost been par for the course to have a fire in the room. By then, NOTHING would have surprised me.

The most frustrating part of the entire experience occurred when I went down to the lobby to check out. When the girl asked how everything was, I explained that it was less than satisfactory. She went to get the manager. This time it was a woman who came to speak to me. She explained that she had heard about our problems and hoped the expensive champagne had made everything better. She made me feel that if I wasn't fully satisfied, I must be a very inconsiderate clod.

I asked if we were not supposed to receive souvenir champagne glasses that we could keep. She said that although they were part of the package, they must have run out of them. She then left. I asked the girl at the counter if that meant we would not receive the glasses. She went and got the manager again. The manager grudgingly phoned someone and told me they would be down shortly. She left again. Five minutes later, two glasses were brought down and plopped in front of me. No, sorry, nothing. I am confident I would not have received them if I had not reminded them that they were part of the "Romance Package."

I was handed the bill and was most surprised to see I was charged $9 for parking. When I questioned this, I was told that there was supposed to be valet parking and I should have asked for it when I arrived. I told her I thought she should have reminded me when

I first came. I inquired why I should have to pay for the parking, especially since I parked it myself. She agreed to take it off the bill.

If any of these occurrences had happened in isolation, I could understand. However, I believe you can see that this comedy of errors made our 25th anniversary most memorable in a very negative way. The couple from the movie *Out of Towners* had nothing on us. I left feeling ripped off. I do not mind paying a fair price, but I expect appropriate service. The Blue-Ribbon guarantee they so proudly displayed should more suitably have been written on toilet paper.

I did send a letter to the hotel stating all of the things I mentioned above. I never heard back from them. Now that we are getting close to the big 50th anniversary, my mind is beginning to formulate a plan as to how we can make this a memorable occasion. One option would be to return to the Delta. What do you think?

We Had Three Children; One of Each

Whenever people ask me how many children we have, I always reply, "Three; one of each." Of course, I then have to explain what I mean is that each of them is unique and completely different. There is an axiom which states, "nature abhors a vacuum." I have found this applies to families as well. Each child has skills and talents that make them unique in a certain way. Once a particular niche has been filled, it seems that the next child inherently knows they need to excel at something different.

That would be very true of our family. Our oldest daughter, Andrea, immediately took on the role of "boss." Everything came quickly and easily to her, and it was not long before she realized how much more fun it was when she was the one in control. We were amazed at how she started to show an interest in talking at a very early age. We spent one year teaching her to speak and the next 17 trying to get her to stop.

Andrea was a fantastic scholar who was reading by the time she was four years old. She was a keener who loved school and always excelled in every subject. There was no question in her or our minds that she would eventually be going to university.

Of the three children, she presented me with the most interesting dilemma I faced as a parent and principal. She was 17 years old and came to me to ask if I would buy some alcoholic beverages for her to take to a party. She went on to logically explain that if I didn't purchase it, she would have to find someone, perhaps that she didn't even know, to buy it for her. My conundrum was what would people think if they found out the school principal was buying alcohol for his underage daughter.

After some soul searching, I realized that not every child trusted their parents enough to ask such a question. It didn't hurt that she had never given us an ounce of trouble, and I trusted her completely. I bought her a six-pack of coolers. That was the first and only time she ever asked. Thinking back, it was probably just a test to see if I would do it.

By the time our son, Dustin was born four years later, Andrea had perfected the art of speech and debate. She took on the role of not only talking for herself but also for her brother. It seemed we were constantly working through an interpreter, and for the longest time, we were apprehensive that he might never learn how to speak.

Dusty quickly learned that the way he could shine without talking was in sports. He was always fast and agile. Even though he was not as big as many of his opponents, he was the proverbial mosquito who was relentless in his pursuit. By the time the opponent figured out where he was, he had already moved somewhere else.

I don't remember a sport Dustin didn't love or didn't excel in. The one thing we never had to teach him was how to be competitive. This became obvious the first time at the age of eight when he and I ran in our initial 10 kilometers race together in Lethbridge. It was halfway through the race when I spotted another runner, about Dustin's age, attempting to pass us.

As Dustin lowered his shoulder and body checked the runner off the trail, I knew it was time to have "the talk" about sportsmanship. An interesting aside to this story is that the young lad he body checked was the son of the doctor who delivered Dustin.

Our youngest daughter, Courtney, was our little rebel. It started on the day of her birth. She refused to come out during her delivery, so the doctor had to use forceps, which did not endear her to her mother. In reality, the umbilical cord was too short, and the placenta kept pulling her back as Irene was trying to push her out.

Courtney always was a social butterfly. She loved everyone, and they all loved her. When it came to school, good grades did not come easily. This was generally more a case of her being more worried about who she would be playing with after school instead of how to factor a polynomial. Interestingly enough, over the years, she developed such excellent work habits that she found university easier than either of her siblings.

Courtney ended up being the only child who followed her father into education. She had the personality, patience, and perseverance vital for teaching. We knew at the age of five that she would become an educator.

We found her downstairs, with her dolls all lined up side by side on the couch. She was holding a toothpick in each hand. We watched as she approached each doll and gently parted the doll's hair using the toothpicks. When we finally asked what she was doing, we were told, in a very matter-of-fact way, that she was checking for head lice just like they do at school.

The Dreaded "C"

It is human nature to want to live "forever." As mere mortals, it is hard for us to think that at some point in time, we will cease to exist. Deep down, we are aware that it will happen, but there is always the hope it won't happen to us for a very long time.

When death steps up and gets in your face, it is terrifying, and everyone reacts differently. Let me share a story about someone who looked death in the eye and used her faith and positivity to beat it.

The date was May 2, 2004. The day started like any other typical day. I went off to work while Irene drove to Lethbridge for her annual mammogram results. This is when she found out that the lumps in her breast were malignant. I cannot imagine the fear and apprehension she endured as the doctor explained that he would schedule surgery within the week.

I don't remember very much about that day, as it was probably a case of purposely trying to forget those things that we refuse to admit are real. Before this devastating news, we were all preparing to celebrate the graduation of our youngest daughter, Courtney, from high school.

Within a week of receiving the shocking news, Irene was in surgery, and the mastectomy was performed. It was, in retrospect, a blessing that we didn't have time to think about all the ramifications. Our lives had forever changed, and things were happening that were beyond our control.

The surgery was deemed a success as it appeared that while the tumors had metastasized, they had only traveled to a couple of lymph nodes under the arm. With any luck, the early diagnosis and surgery would be enough to stop the cancer from spreading. Being somewhat naïve about the treatment process, I was elated that things were over and we could finally get back to normal.

Little did I realize that the painful journey had just begun. It wasn't long before chemo treatments were scheduled. The prognosis was that six sessions would be necessary. These had to be spread out over several weeks to ensure the body had time to recover from the effects of the caustic chemicals used to fight the disease.

To be blunt, the purpose of chemo is simple. The treatment is to put enough poison into the body to kill the cancer cells without actually killing the host. It was a "good news, bad news" situation for each treatment. While we knew the chemicals would help, we also quickly discovered the horrible side effects that accompanied the treatment.

It was not uncommon for Irene to become physically ill before, during, and after her sessions. A day or two later, when the chemicals' effects kicked in, it was usual for her to sleep the day away. While she seldom complained, I knew the pain she was suffering was extreme. Gradually her body would get stronger, and eventually, she was ready for another "hit" of chemo.

The most challenging part of the whole process was when her hair started to fall out. Rather than let this happen, she took control of the situation. She immediately booked an appointment at the hairdresser and had her head shaved. She was not going to let this invader intrude upon her happiness any further. In support, the kids and I gave her the following letter.

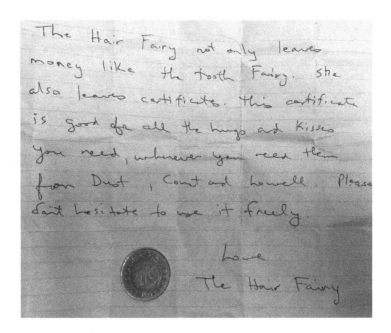

The Hair Fairy not only leaves money like the tooth Fairy. She also leaves certificate. This certificate is good for all the hugs and kisses you need, whenever you need them from Dust, Court and Lowell. Please don't hesitate to use it freely.

Love
The Hair Fairy

Now that our grandchildren get $5 each time they lose a tooth, I wonder if the Hair Fairy is keeping up with inflation.

This story has a happy ending because Irene has now been cancer-free for 17 years. While the thought of it coming back never goes away, we thank God for every day that it stays in remission. There is no doubt that her faith in the Lord and the power of positive thought were the driving forces behind her beating this ugly opponent.

It was several years later that an incident occurred which had a significant impact on me. I was sitting in the car, waiting while Irene was shopping for something. I remember looking in the rear-view mirror and seeing a couple across the street. She was bent over and vomiting while he stood helplessly by her side. My first thought was, "it is only 10:00 in the morning, and those two are already drunk". Talk about the ignorance of making assumptions. When I read the sign above the couple, it hit me between the eyes. The couple was just getting ready to enter the cancer treatment center.

Gambling Never Pays

I have never enjoyed gambling. The joy of winning never seemed to dominate the fear of losing. When I was growing up, there was not much excess money around. Don't get me wrong, we never went without our basic needs and generally more. It was just so apparent that our parents came from humble beginnings, and they never took anything for granted.

My dislike of gambling was not genetic. Dad enjoyed his nights out with the guys to drink and play cards. Sometimes this even got in the way of our going to the drive-inn theatre. It did not occur very often, but when it did, Dad faced the wrath of the four of us who were upset about not getting our weekly feed of fish and chips.

Later in life, Mom and Dad would often drive to Nevada to gamble in Reno or Jackpot. They never won the "big one," but I also doubt they ever lost very much. The thrill seemed to be in getting away and enjoying the cheap food and drinks that came with the gambling.

The one thing that contributed the most to my dislike of losing goes back to one of my yearly holidays with my Aunt and Uncle. One summer, they took me to a carnival with rides, food, and games of chance. My parents always left me with an allowance that I could use to buy things such as treats and souvenirs over the week that I was visiting.

While the carnival had many barkers calling out to get our attention, there was one booth that piqued my interest. They had the most amazing prizes, although I have no recollection of what they were. To win a prize, you had to throw a small hoop and have it land on the neck of a long-necked bottle. He made it look so easy during the demonstration.

Aunt Alma, who acted as my treasurer, gave me enough money to play a few games. I came close but couldn't win. I remember this guy saying how sure he was that next time I would WIN. I remember pleading for more money for a couple more tries. Aunt Alma knew I wouldn't win, and I also know she gave me the money to teach me a lesson.

I ended up blowing my whole week's allowance and had nothing to show for it. I didn't suffer that much because Uncle Alex made sure I got all the things I would have, even if I had still had my own money. The lesson was indeed learned, and I will never forget the hopeless feeling of having "lost it all." It was then that I realized I would never again let that happen to me.

Fast forward 30 years, and we are taking our kids to the annual Lethbridge exhibition. As we walked by the many booths, Dusty spotted the "Ole Fishing Hole." It involved using a long fishing pole with a magnet attached to the end. The object was to catch one of the many disks floating in the water. On the bottom of the disk, under the water, the name of a particular prize was listed. Prizes varied from cheap, worthless trinkets to the grand prize, a 4-foot stuffed dog. Dusty figured that he had to have the dog.

After some tears and whining, I flashed back to when Aunt Alma taught me a life lesson. I decided this was the perfect time to do the same for my son. I made him use his own money, and he gleefully grabbed one of the poles. The thing about this game was that once a fish was caught, the game was over. I am sure Dusty wanted to relish the experience by hovering the magnet over many different fish before actually deciding on the one lucky fish that would be hooked. Well, it didn't quite work out that way.

As soon as he put the magnet close to the water, one of the disks immediately stuck, and the fish was caught. Game OVER. For me, this was a good thing as I speculated that the lesson would quickly be learned, and we could move on to other things. Was I wrong!! You guessed it. Of all the hundreds of disks he could have caught, the one he hooked read "GRAND PRIZE." I sure taught him a lesson that day.

And the Winner Is …

After graduating from the University of Calgary in 1976, I took a teaching position with the Calgary Separate School System. I began my teaching career at the St. Margaret Junior High School, located in the Brentwood area of NW Calgary. After three years, I transferred to St. Martha School in Marlborough Park, NE, where I taught for another three years.

During that time, we lived in the Beddington Heights area in the NW. The point I am making here is that I did not live close to the school where I taught, so there was a lot of driving back and forth to work each day. I needed to have a reliable vehicle to get me through the many miles I put on each week.

During the drives, I would listen to CHQR radio, which played the music of the 60s and 70s. The radio station decided to sponsor a contest, where the winner would receive a brand new 1980 Chevrolet HHR Retro Utility Vehicle. Contestants were encouraged to send in a story of why they deserved a new car. Each day, one story was read on the radio and qualified for one of the 50 spots available for the contest. I decided it was worth a shot, so I submitted the following story:

I believe I deserve a new Chevy HHR to help offset the years of suffering and trauma that were caused as a result of owning a 1977 Volkswagen Rabbit. This car had a bad habit of vapor locking and stalling in heavy traffic. My friend, Tom, offered a solution that was so absurd, I thought he was setting me up for a joke. It wasn't long after, during rush hour traffic on Crowchild Trail, that my car started chugging and gasping before it stopped dead. I got out in the middle of traffic and took off the gas cap. I got down on my knees and cupped my hands around the filling spout. I sealed the spout with my mouth and blew as hard as possible into the gas tank.

You would not believe some of the lewd comments complete strangers would yell out their window as they slowly drove by. When I put the cap back on and turned the ignition, the car started immediately. I could never figure out the logic of when or why it would choose to stall. Each time, as soon as I blew into the gas tank, the problem was fixed. There were, however, two unfortunate side effects that occurred. The first was that it took the rest of the day to get rid of the gas taste. Secondly, it took a lot of scrubbing to wash off the black ring around my mouth, formed after pressing my face against the dirty gas spout.

This was a true story. I was happily surprised, one day, as I was driving to work and I heard the radio announcer read my story on the air. Since this was before cell phones, I had to wait until I got home after work to listen to their message about how I had qualified for the contest. The message explained how all 50 entrants would meet at the Chevy dealership, close to the Planetarium, downtown. I was about the 30th qualifier, so I had to wait an additional month before the contest was filled.

All the contestants assembled on a Saturday at 8:00 am inside the dealership. There was electricity in the air, with everyone dreaming of driving home a brand-new car that day. The radio station personnel treated us like royalty and the day began with a breakfast buffet of eggs, bacon, pancakes, and all the fixings. We were live on the air, and throughout the meal, announcers would come around and record the reactions and excitement that was mounting.

There were some pretty amazing prizes available. Along with the new car, there was a trip to Europe, a trip to Disneyland, and a trip to the Maritimes. They had donations which included a snowblower, stereo systems, and even some appliances. The good news was that everyone received a prize. The bad news was that the expensive ones were left to the last ten survivors. The way the contest worked was that it featured a reverse draw. All 50 names were put in a barrel, and one at a time, a name was pulled out. Once your name was pulled, you were eliminated from the competition. So, you did NOT want to hear your name called.

While I wanted that new car so badly, I couldn't get my hopes up because I knew that would be the kiss of death. My biggest fear was being the first person drawn. The entire contest was spread out over a couple of hours. The announcers "milked" as much air time as they could, all the while prolonging the suspense. As each name was drawn, the disappointed contestant walked up to the front, where they received their prize.

The first ten names were called, and I was thrilled my name was still in contention. When the next ten names were announced, once again, no Lowell was heard. As they approached the end of the next 10, I was beginning to think maybe I had a chance after all. That WAS the kiss of death. With 21 names remaining, mine was drawn, and I was DONE.

I remember the walk up to the front seeming to take hours. I was disappointed and depressed. My prize was a CD by the group Coldplay. I had never heard of them, so I gave it away on the way back when someone said they were their favourite group. That person had probably never heard of them either, but it was a great way to get a free CD.

The rest of the draws were pretty anticlimactic until it got down to the final five. By that time, the worst prize you could get was a fridge, and the best was the car, with various trips in between. The car ended up going to a young couple. From their excitement, it was obviously going to a deserving home.

It is not every day you get a one in 50 chance to win a new car, and while I did not get to drive it home, it was still a day I will never forget.

Sports and Recreation

Scuba Dooby Doo

As a child, swimming was never my favourite thing to do, and swimming lessons were the WORST. The last thing I felt the urge to do was to swim 70 lengths of a swimming pool to complete one mile. If this was one length per day over 70 days, I could live with it.

Why would anyone purposely jump in the deep end, fully dressed, to see if they could tread water for five minutes? I must admit, as a youngster in the early 60s, nothing seemed more exciting than watching Lloyd Bridges in the action-adventure television series "Sea Hunt."

We lived in Calgary during the early years of our marriage, and Irene worked in the French lab at Mount Royal College. One day, she came home and told me that the College offered a night class in scuba diving. I couldn't help but dive at the chance to get certified.

The cost was $100 and involved 14 hours of classroom instruction, 10 hours in the pool, and an open water test in Lake Minnewanka, outside of Banff. This all seemed a little excessive to me as I couldn't imagine how difficult it was to put on an air tank, jump in the water, and swim around. Being a teacher during the day, the last thing I wanted to do was sit in a classroom at night and listen to someone else talk. I was, definitely, not ready for what lay ahead.

I had no idea we would be studying the "Law." That being, Boyle's Law, Charles' Law, Henry's Law, and Dalton's Law. Without going into all the complicated physics involved, the bottom line is this:

"You have to know your altitude above sea level, how far you go down in the water, and how long you stay under." Make a mistake with any of these, and **"You get the bends."** This happens when nitrogen bubbles form in your circulation system and block tiny blood vessels. It can lead to heart attacks, strokes, ruptured blood vessels in the lungs, joint pain, and sometimes death. Doesn't that sound like FUN?

It didn't take me long to figure out why we needed so much time in the classroom. Being a science teacher, the physics part for me was no problem. My struggles started when we jumped in the pool for our confined water training.

The first thing a diver must learn to do is equalize their ear pressure. Just by swimming down to the bottom of the deep end in a pool, you can feel the pressure exerted from the water into your ears. If you don't clear your ears before attempting a descent into the water, the pain becomes extreme, and you can burst your eardrum.

By pinching the nose, closing your mouth, and gently blowing out, you will feel a pop in your ears, just like when you go up or down in an airplane. By opening the normally closed Eustachian tubes, you allow higher-pressured air from your throat to enter your middle ears, and the discomfort is immediately relieved. This is why you never scuba dive when you have a cold and your sinuses are plugged. The excess mucous makes it impossible to clear your ears.

Once we mastered ear clearing, the next problem was something I had not even imagined. When we breathe normally, we don't think about it, but we inhale through our nose and mouth. The most challenging part of our training was learning how to breathe through our mouth only and not inhaling through our nose. You breathe air in through the regulator in your mouth and expel it back out the same way it came in. Your nose is enclosed in a mask, and if you try to breathe in through it, the mask sucks up to your face.

Once you teach your nose not to breathe, life becomes "easier." The training involved swimming around the bottom of the pool without a mask while breathing from our tanks. There is nothing funnier than watching as the other divers come shooting up to the surface after having inhaled a nose full of water. Unfortunately, it was not nearly as funny when I did it. Slowly and with a lot of practice and inhalation of pool water, we all learned how to breathe correctly.

Clearing your mask is another skill that takes some practice to perfect. Even though you have your mask on before entering the water, at some point, water does seep in around the seal, or something can happen where your entire mask floods. When you are 100 feet under, you don't want to have to end your dive by going to the surface to clear your mask. The trick is to look up and place your hands on either side of your mask. By keeping the seal at the top and pulling the bottom away from your face, you can blow air out your nose. This pushes all the water out. It works like magic.

Once we had completed the 10 hours in the pool, it was time for the confined water test. We had to throw our tanks, mask, and flippers into the deep end of the pool. Our task was to dive in and get fully dressed without resurfacing. The first thing to do was turn on your air and get the regulator in your mouth to breathe. Next, we had to put on our mask and clear the water out.

While this was happening, our instructor was suited up and down there, waiting for us. He was a silent shark, waiting to inflict pain upon us. During the test, he was NOT our friend. While we were clearing our mask, he would turn off the air on our tanks. We had to find the knob to turn the air back on. Meanwhile, he is pulling your mask off so that it fills up with water.

While this may sound cruel, we needed to learn how to react appropriately if something untoward should happen while we are diving out in nature. When he was convinced that we would not panic, he let us slip the tanks onto our back, put on our flippers, and swim away. You don't appreciate the importance of this until you actually find yourself in a real-life situation.

Sudden Shrinkage

It was mid-October when we arrived at Lake Minnewanka for the final leg of our open water training. Minnewanka is a glacial lake located in the Banff National Park. The lake is 21 kilometers long and 142 meters deep. The lake was not frozen over, but there were snow and ice on the banks. The temperature of glacial lakes, summer or winter, is COLD. It seldom gets above 5 Celsius.

On the surface, Lake Minnewanka looks like most other lakes, but many visitors don't realize that underneath the lake are the remains of a ghost town. From 1886 – 1941, nearby Calgary visitors would flock to this popular summer resort known as Minnewanka Landing. During the Second World War, the city of Calgary started to boom. When the growing metropolis became desperate for electrical power, a new dam was built.

This dam raised the water level by over 98 feet and engulfed the entire town. The wooden structures, immersed in the cold water, survived quite well and remained intact. It is still possible to observe house and hotel foundations, piers, an oven, a chimney, a cellar, bridge pilings, and sidewalks. Since we were "rookie divers," we would have to come back another day to explore the ghost town. It was time for us to get tested for certification.

There are two kinds of diving suits that can be worn during scuba diving. One is called a wet suit, and the other is a dry suit. I probably don't have to tell you how they got their respective names. The most challenging part of diving is getting the wetsuit on your body. It must be very tight-fitting to ensure the cold water is not continually flowing through. The best way to describe dressing up in a wet suit is to imagine trying to force too much meat into an incredibly tiny casing, creating sausage links. After a great deal of wiggling and twisting and with our wetsuit finally, in place, we entered the lake.

The first thing we quickly noticed was the ice-cold water entering from the wrist and ankle openings, filling the entire suit with a layer of frigid water. Once you regain your breath and stop hyperventilating, the good news was that it didn't take long for our bodies to warm the water to a point where it was almost comfortable.

The first leg of our testing regime did not involve the use of our air tanks. Using only our snorkel to breathe, we had to make a 15-minute swim on the surface out to a buoy where the water's depth was around 15 feet deep. Once at the buoy, we had to take a breath and swim down to the bottom to pick up a rock. The rock was proof to the instructor that we had indeed made it to the bottom. Not only do wetsuits provide warmth, but they are also very buoyant and help you stay afloat.

Getting down to the bottom is not just a matter of holding your breath and dropping down. The only way to submerge is to point your head down and swim as though you were being chased by a hungry shark. After several attempts, I finally surfaced with a rock and swam back to complete phase two of the testing.

With our air tanks now strapped to our backs, we swam along with the instructor out to a point where the water was about 40 feet deep. To compensate for the wetsuit buoyancy, we had to wear a weighted belt to keep us from floating up. Along with the instructor, we all swam to the bottom, where we waited while each student was tested.

Forty feet might not seem far down, but you have to realize most of the visible spectrum of light disappears after 30 feet. At that depth, there is no colour, and even crystal-clear water looks dark and grey.

When you look up, all you see is the air bubbles you just blew out, rising slowly up until they disappear.

To start the test, we had to take the regulator out of our mouth and hold it in our hand. We had to slowly use our fins to begin our ascent to the surface. The definitive term here is SLOWLY. I can remember diving into the deep end of a pool and then swimming like a madman to get to the top for a breath, thinking I was going to die. How did the instructor expect us to swim slowly up from 40 feet down? Had he lost his mind?

As I started to rise, using the speed of my air bubbles as a guide, I remember waiting for the panic that would hit me once I felt my oxygen run out. As I kept swimming up, I kept waiting. I reached the top, and amazingly, I wasn't gasping for air.

When you go under the water, the air becomes pressurized in your tank. So, when you breathe it, you are breathing compressed air. As you swim up, the air expands due to the lower pressure, and when you reach the top, you have the same amount of air as when you were on the bottom. This is why you NEVER hold your breath when you are going up. The expanding air can do damage to your lungs and other body parts. Also, there is that other problem called the "bends" to worry about.

The day was a success, with us being dubbed Certified Scuba Divers. SCUBA is an acronym for Self Contained Underwater Breathing Apparatus, and we were now qualified to dive anywhere in the world. Although I have never returned to Lake Minnewanka, I will tell you next about my diving experiences in Waterton and Hawaii.

Things That Take Your Breath Away

As we found ourselves approaching the 10-year mark of marital bliss, I decided I would like to surprise Irene with a trip to Hawaii. I began to search through books and brochures, looking for all the "Must Sees." Remember, the internet was not yet invented. One article, in particular, intrigued me as it described the fantastic undersea world that you could only access by traveling "under" the water. As an angler would say, "I was hooked."

It had been several years since my scuba certification, so I decided I had to reacquaint myself with the sport of diving before I decided to jump into the Pacific Ocean. There was a "dive club" in Lethbridge, and they were advertising a weekend diving experience in Waterton Lakes. We drove up on Friday night because we needed to spend the night at altitude. This would allow our bodies' nitrogen levels to stabilize so our dive tables and how long we could stay underwater would be accurate.

On Saturday morning, it was a short drive from our motel to Emerald Bay, one of the most popular spots for divers in Waterton. An old paddle wheeler, the "Gertrude," was built in the early 1900s and lies on the bottom of the bay at a depth of 20 meters. While it was not the best time of the year to dive, as the water was a little murky, it was fun to do a little exploration of the ruins of the boat.

All of the metal parts are still intact, and much of the wood is still visible. The biggest surprise was how many fish there were swimming around.

After spending 45 minutes there, it was time to have some lunch and let some of the excess nitrogen leave our bodies before the next dive. In the afternoon, we drove across town to the beach at the end of the campground. From this point, the lake gets deep, very quickly, and we spent the time hunting along the shoreline for fishing hooks. These were plentiful as many anglers' lines had snagged on the various rocks and snapped off. After this second dive, we were done for the day.

The next day took us up to Cameron Lake. The drive involves a long, steep incline, and once you get to the Lake, the view is spectacular. The water is crystal clear and COLD. It is glacier-fed, and even though it was summer, the water's temperature was a single digit. The majority of the lake is shallow enough that the colours were spectacular. If you remember, previously, I indicated that below 30 feet, the visible light spectrum disappears, so everything looks grey.

It was during this dive that one of the most bizarre and surreal experiences of my life occurred. I was looking around the bottom, and when I looked up, an entire school of hundreds of fish was swimming slowly towards me. The school had some of the larger fish in the lead and others, bringing up the rear. They seemed to be the guards. In between, there were fish of all sizes. As long as I didn't breathe out too quickly, creating a bunch of bubbles, the fish didn't seem disturbed by my presence. They swam slowly around me and continued on their way. Talk about having your breath taken away. This was the highlight of just about anything I have ever done as far as recreation is concerned.

For our last dive in the afternoon, we drove a short distance out of the townsite and stopped at the river. We did a river dive, which involved floating slowly with the river current propelling us along. After an hour, we ended up near the East entrance to the park. The river dive was totally unique in that it involved very little swimming, and we just floated along with the current. Once again, there were many fish hooks and broken lines telling stories of snagged anglers.

Fast forward to February of the same year, and we found ourselves touching down in Honolulu, where we were greeted by sunshine, leis, and Pina Coladas. One of the first things I did was book a dive trip for later in the week. As a warm-up, I spent one-afternoon snorkeling in Hanauma Bay. You probably noticed I didn't say "we." Irene does not even put her head under in the shower, so she relaxed on the beach while I explored under the water.

It was incredible to see all the colours and different types of aquatic life. Our bartender from the previous night had explained the intricacies of snorkeling and how to feed the fish. As everyone knows, bartenders know everything, and the longer you drink, the more expert they become.

I learned that the easiest thing to feed fish was bread or buns. The trick was to squeeze the bun, so it squished out between your fingers, and the fish would nibble at the back of your hand and NOT bite your fingers. This worked exceptionally well, and the fish quickly discovered where they could get a free meal. It was great fun until I suddenly realized that most of the smaller fish had been chased off, and the larger fish that were now eating had more prominent teeth.

When my big day to jump into the Pacific arrived, I was pumped. Our party of six boarded a small dive boat which transported us towards our dive site. We put on our equipment and jumped into the water. I couldn't help but look around and see that we were surrounded by open water. When I attempted to submerge underwater, I quickly discovered I couldn't breathe. I checked my air and confirmed it was turned on. I tried again, but there was no air coming out of my mouthpiece.

I informed the guide that my tank must have been empty. I'm not sure if it was the panic in my eyes or the sweat running down my face, but the guide had me climb back into the boat, where I was told to breathe slowly and deeply. This was the first and only time I ever experienced "hyperventilation." While this could have been the end of my dive, the instructor was patient, and we slowly worked through the anxiety attack, and eventually, I did participate in the dive. I was unable to catch lobsters like some of the experienced divers did, but at least I got to observe some moray eels, sea turtles, and the coral reefs. Looking back, it was another example of how fear can paralyze you, but if you can work through it, it is definitely worth the effort.

True Grit

The Victoria Day long weekend in May has always been a memorable date on the Gregorian Calendar for our family. For those with a penchant for the great outdoors, it marks the transition from winter and our confinement inside to Spring and the freedom to enjoy Mother Nature in all her natural splendor and glory. For those who are blessed with a green thumb, it is the best time to plant their gardens in hopes of harvesting a rich bounty of fruit and vegetables in a couple of months.

For us, it was the time to take our RVs out of winter storage and venture out for the first weekend of the camping season. Anyone who has ventured out this weekend knows you should expect anything as far as the weather is concerned. It can fluctuate from hot and sunny to cold and even snowy, often on the same weekend.

Our destination of choice for this weekend was always "The Creek," or more specifically, The Meadow at Caven Creek. The Creek was about a 3-hour drive from Bow Island, which meant we could leave after work on Friday and arrive there well before dark that night. We could get in two full days of camping before having to return home on Victoria Day Monday.

To access our secluded piece of Heaven, we drove through Kikomun Provincial Park in BC and continued along a logging trail to a small clearing situated on Caven Creek. Although we would sometimes have another group staying in the area, it was remote enough to feel like we were getting away from it all. The year was 1980 of this particular Victoria Day Long Weekend.

The goal of this weekend was twofold. First, it was to ensure everything in the RV was in good working order and ready for a long season of camping ahead. The second was to catch enough rainbow trout for our first fish fry of the year. This meant that Saturday and Sunday were devoted entirely to catching enough fish for our inaugural feast of the season.

The "men" were charged with taking our equipment out to the creek, where we would ply our skills to outsmart the fish. The gatherers would stay at the camp to keep the fires burning and take care of all the little, future hunters and gatherers. After a grueling day of casting and reeling, the catch was cleaned and prepared for our evening meal.

There is nothing easier to prepare or tastier to eat than a nine-inch rainbow trout. They have no scales, so cleaning simply involved an incision to the underbelly from the tail to the head. Cutting the head off from the top left the entrails intact, and all the organs and intestines came out in one deft pull.

When the remaining carcasses were floured, along with some salt and pepper, and fried in butter or bacon grease, you ended up with a crisp, golden brown nugget of heaven. By nibbling the meat along the back, the two fillets could be pulled off each side of the vertebrae. This left the entire skeleton and bones in one piece, ready to be discarded. The boneless, succulent fillets were primed and ready to be devoured with no threat of choking from a bone. Once supper had been consumed, it was time for several hours of sitting around the campfire. Drinking, laughing, and telling stories followed until it was time to retire so we could do it all again the next day.

It was a beautiful Sunday morning when the "event" occurred. At the time, I had no idea of its significance. I was out fishing on the creek, enjoying the radiant sunshine and hoping the fish would cooperate. I was lost in thought when I distinctly remember hearing a rumbling in the sky to the South. This was not unusual since we often had thunderstorms suddenly appear out of nowhere. When I looked up, there was not a cloud in the sky, and I didn't think much more about it.

That night, things went pretty much as usual. We stoked up the fire and sat around, drinks in hand, and told stories about the "big" one that got away. Our drink of choice was rye and coke at night, beer during the day. When we got to the bottom of our drinks, I remember spitting out a mouthful of sediment. My thought process was that I had drunk too much and used a dirty glass. That could only mean I had consumed enough, and it was time for bed.

When we got up the following day, it was a sight we would never forget. If it had been white, we would have known it had snowed overnight. Everything was covered by a coat of grey dust: our camp-site, the vehicles, the trees, the ground, EVERYTHING. Although you could see the sun trying to shine through, the sky was black.

We had no clue as to what had happened. We debated a nuclear holocaust or forest fires that had caused the ash to blow in. It is hard not to think about the worst possible case scenario. These were the times of the Cold War, and we had gone through the days of "bomb drills" in the schools. We would practice having the whole class crawl under their desk and put their arms over their heads. Seriously, was that going to protect us during an atomic explosion?

This was the time before cell phones, and where we camped, we did not have any access to radio reception. Since we were leaving that day, anyway, we quickly packed up the units and headed out to find whether, indeed, the world had ended. When we got to Kikomun, we stopped at the store to see if they were any the wiser. It was then that we discovered Mount Saint Helens had exploded, and the ensuing volcano had spread its ash hundreds of miles away.

We did not suffer any of the trauma that many areas closer to the epicenter did. Other than some damage to carburetors and other internal combustion engines, the biggest problem we had to deal with was the mess and cleanup for weeks afterward. In the end, we did learn that while volcanic ash is not poisonous, it will never replace ice when it comes to mixing a good drink.

Getting High

Even from a young age, I don't remember being afraid of heights. Climbing was a big part of what we did every day. Unlike the children of today, we climbed trees. Poplar trees had an excellent structure for honing our skills of ascent. We would often climb as high as we could and imagine ourselves looking down at the world like only a bird could.

It is a good thing most of the old wooden grain elevators are no longer standing. To us, they were the early jungle gyms. They were constructed with 8-inch x 8-inch beams running around the entire structure. Every 10 feet up, there was a new walkway level we could access. As we developed into better mountain goats, we eventually summoned up the courage to do our walkabout at the very top.

The average elevator was 122 feet tall. If we take off the top 22 feet, that still left us 100 feet above the ground. The last thing we ever thought about was what might happen if we fell. Fortunately, none of us ever did. We would spend hours walking around the elevator, often playing tag. The rush we experienced always made us feel like the *King of the World*.

When I reached adolescence, my fascination with heights continued. Anyone living in Bow Island knows the tallest structure in town is the water tower. It is at least as high as the grain elevators were, and it was not uncommon for us, on a Saturday night, to take along a couple of refreshments and climb the ladder up to the top of the tower.

There was a platform at the top that circled the tower, and we would sit up there, contemplating life, towering above the rest of the world. No one ever accused an adolescent of being bright, and this is another one of those things that I am not proud of. At the time, it seemed like a good idea, and no one ever fell or got hurt in the climb.

There were two other experiences where I remember feeling queasy, looking down at the ground far below. The first was when we took a trip up the CN Tower in Toronto. When you exited the elevator, you stepped out onto a metal, mesh floor you could see through. I can remember looking down and feeling like I might lose my lunch.

The other time was when we traveled up the Calgary Tower for breakfast. We were seated next to the windows to enjoy the sights as the tower slowly revolved. At some point in the meal, we heard the whine of sirens below. When we looked down, we could see the flashing lights of several fire engines directly below the tower. There was some sort of minor smoke incident in the kitchen that involved an alarm being called in. While nothing came of the situation, it was still pretty unnerving to be up that high and wondering how you might get down alive.

Always Be Nice to the Person Who Packs Your Parachute

Being the slow learner that I am, it was many years later when my courage was tested in a way that can't be described unless you have been there. A friend purchased three passes for a first-time sky jump package, and since there was no way that he would use them, he gave them to me.

I don't have a death wish, but as you can see from earlier adventures, I was not averse to getting as close to the edge as possible. I was now faced with finding two other victims to accompany me in jumping out of a perfectly good airplane. The first was pretty easy, as my 16-year-old son thought this was something he wanted to do. When he talked to his 17-year-old cousin Ryan, it was a done deal. I will never forget the words of my sister, Wendy, when she looked me straight in the eye and said, "If anything happens to Ryan, don't bother coming home." She wasn't smiling.

The big day finally arrived, and we were off to Didsbury, where we were involved in a nine-hour training session. Our jump was the real deal where we would fall all by ourselves. We would not be attached to an instructor. I can barely remember a few of the things we learned. For example, they told us more people died from touching a powerline on the way down than from their parachute not opening. This was certainly encouraging news. They also told us there was a reserve chute we could use if the primary chute malfunctioned. The instructor assured us that in most cases, one of the two chutes should open.

When it came time for the jump, we were suited up with our parachutes and marched boldly towards the plane to board. Describing our vehicle as a plane may be understating it a little. It was small and barely held the pilot, the instructor, and the three of us jumpers. The aircraft had been gutted, and the only thing left was the seat for the pilot. The door to the plane had been taken off entirely, so it was not in the way when we exited the plane.

I can remember thinking, just before boarding that if I am the last one to jump, I still have the option of chickening out. If I came to my senses, I could just stay on the plane and leave the excitement to the kids. My plan was quickly shattered when the instructor told us we would be lining up to board with the heaviest person going in last and jumping out first. This was so that it was easier for the plane to circle and gain altitude for the next jumper. I quickly sucked in my gut, but it was pretty apparent neither one of the skinny teens was going in last.

So, the three of us had to wiggle in and kneel back to front with the other two guys, facing the instructor at the front of the plane. To picture this, think sardines. The instructor was kneeling, facing us right next to the open door. To keep our minds off what lay ahead, the Instructor had us singing songs and yelling aloud because you could hardly hear over the wind rushing past the open door.

Before I knew it, the end drew near. The instructor looked at me, smiled, and said, "You're up." I crawled slowly up to the open door, and as instructed, I swung my left foot out and placed it on the small foothold just outside the door. The instructor helped me reach up with my left hand and grab onto the plane's wing. I had to reach over and grab the wing with my other hand. When I did this, my foot came off the pedal, and there I was, hanging on to the wing with my feet fluttering behind me.

The only thing between me and the drop to the ground below was my fingers clamped onto the wing. On the first jump, you are not allowed to freefall, and we were attached to a line connected to a pilot chute. When we released our grip from the plane, the instructor threw out the little chute, which immediately opened and proceeded to open our chute.

I can vividly remember thinking, "I am going to die if I let go." When my fingers finally succumbed to the force of gravity, all I can remember is seeing the plane instantly disappear from my sight. I also remember looking up and seeing my chute open and feeling the jerk that announced I was going to live after all. We had a headset, and the controller on the ground would tell us to turn left or right and guided us down to the spot he wanted us to land. Even though Didsbury was 45 minutes from Calgary, we could see much of the city, and it was a surreal feeling to float slowly downward.

In the end, we all lived to tell the tale. However, I can honestly say I have never been more afraid in my entire life than when I was holding on to that wing, knowing what was about to happen. Would I ever do it again? If we completed five successful jumps, we would be allowed to freefall and open the chute ourselves. I did a couple more jumps a few months later, but maybe I did get a little smarter, as I never got to the point where my existence was dependent upon my ability to open my own parachute.

Lowell's first jump in Didsbury, 1998

Going to the Dogs

In July of 2007, Irene and I attended a superintendent conference in the Yukon. Our schedule allowed us some off-time to explore the sights and sounds of Whitehorse. I read in a brochure about a place called the Muktuk Kennels. They offered a Hike and Howl program where you could spend the day "Going to the Dogs," literally. There were 125 dogs on the compound, each with their private doghouse. They were chained up, but the length of their restraint was enough that they could move around and even jump up on top of their houses. When we arrived, we were greeted by the owner Frank Turner and his wife.

Frank was an active dog musher who participated in a 1609 kilometer race called the Yukon Quest. Each year it is run in the opposite direction, so they either start or stop at Whitehorse and end at Fairbanks, Alaska. To put it in perspective, this is about the distance from Moose Jaw, Saskatchewan, to Vancouver, British Columbia. It is a highly grueling race as the Yukon Quest runs over four different mountain ranges.

Each team starts with 14 dogs and the musher. The race generally takes from 9 to 14 days to complete, depending on the weather. This is approximately 100 miles per day, with only dog power driving you along. Frank won the race in 1995 and is in the Dog Musher Hall of Fame.

The first thing he told us was to go into the compound and meet the dogs. When he saw the panicked look on our faces, he quickly reassured us there wasn't one dog out there we couldn't pet or play with. If the dog didn't want to see us, they would just go inside their doghouse.

I had seen enough movies about the North to know that all mushing dogs were more wolf than dog, and they would tear your arm off if given a chance. This was, of course, because their evil masters would regularly beat those vicious dogs into compliance.

With a great deal of trepidation, we summoned up the courage to enter the dog area. One of the first dogs we walked up to was a colossal husky with piercing blue eyes. I made sure Irene was in front of me in case the dog attacked. I'm kidding. We were side by side, so there was a 50/50 chance as to who would get eaten first.

As we approached, I looked to see if the ears were sticking straight up. I had heard this was one way you could tell if a dog is ready to kill you. When the dog got down and turned onto his back, exposing his underside, I knew this dog wanted nothing more than a good belly rub. We were amazed to discover this was the case with every one of the dogs in the compound. They all loved the attention and were more than happy to play and jump up and lick us.

The stereotype of cruel and inhumane dog mushers and mistreated dog teams was instantly shattered. Frank's philosophy with the dogs is that they all needed to receive a human touch every day of their lives. From the day they were born, the puppies would be held and petted by any number of the helpers who lived and worked at the kennel.

These dogs were loved and cared for from the time they were born until they left for doggie heaven. I immediately realized raising dogs is not that different from raising kids. The best thing we can give either is our undivided love and attention. They both crave a vigorous "belly rub."

While we were walking around the enclosure, we came to one of the pens where they kept the dogs that had given birth to a new litter of puppies. Frank took us inside and gave us each a newly born puppy to cuddle. The puppy I held was a Heinz 57 cross, but she was pure white. Her eyes hadn't opened yet, but she immediately nuzzled against my chest, and I could feel our two hearts beating in unison. I will come back to this puppy in a future story.

Once we had played with the dogs for a few hours, we were exposed to the experience of a dog team. Without any snow around, we didn't take out a sleigh. We took a group of the dogs out for a run. These were all working dogs who needed to exercise every day, and so small groups would be taken out and let loose to run and play outside the compound.

They were not just released to go crazy. As we walked along, Frank would whistle occasionally. The dogs would know they had gone too far away. They would immediately come back closer to the group. I remember thinking if I were going to have effective class-room control, I would need to learn to whistle. It sure worked with the dogs.

The unforgettable day at the kennel ended with a barbeque of several different exotic types of meat. By then, we were so hungry we could have eaten a moose. Oh, wait a minute, we did eat some moose, along with deer and caribou. It would be an understatement to say the Muktuk Kennels' visit was the biggest highlight of our entire trip. To be honest, we didn't know what to expect, but our expectations were blown away.

It was also pretty memorable, on another day, when we went golfing and teed off at 9:00 pm. I was a little leery that we would get all 18 holes in before dark struck. When I realized the sun doesn't set until after 2:00 am, my fears were allayed. I can remember looking up and staring into the bright sun as I attempted to follow an errant drive into the trees. When I checked my wristwatch, I was amazed to see it was 11:30 pm.

As we were leaving Muktuk, we took a couple of minutes to pet and say goodbye to several of the dogs. We thanked Frank for a perfect day and he thanked us for coming to visit. It was obvious from our smiles that we had enjoyed ourselves tremendously. He could tell I was both overwhelmed and overjoyed with the experience. His parting words to me were, "If you ever want to come back in the winter and learn to become a musher, here is my card." And guess what? I did!

Mush and I Don't Mean Porridge

The date is February 13, 2009, and I am standing at the carousel in the Whitehorse Airport, waiting for my luggage to arrive. It has been just over a month since my son and daughter-in-law were married on the beach in Playa del Carmen, Mexico. So, I have gone from sunny and 30 C to snowing and -30 C far too quickly for my body to adapt. I tried to convince them to get married in February so that I could go to the Yukon in January, but you know how unreasonable kids can sometimes be. The one advantage of doing things in this order was that I had a great tan, and it would be easier to find me if I got lost in the snow.

I had decided to grow a beard, not only for warmth but also in the hopes of trying to make this experience as authentic as possible. It is the law that all dog mushers must have a beard. Imagine a lush field of wheat, so thick it looks like a carpet. Imagine that same field after a devastating hail storm goes through. That is precisely what my beard resembled. Patchy with occasional stems sticking out.

The airport was bustling as the Yukon Quest Dog race was happening in a few days. Mushers and spectators from all over the world arrived for the big event. As I was waiting for my luggage, a woman beside me asked if I were a participant in the race. I immediately stroked my beard and thought it worked. I look the part. I don't look like a tourist. Afterward, I thought, I hope she was referring to my being a musher and not one of the dogs.

As I entered the main lobby to exit the airport, I saw a guy who resembled Grizzly Adams, and he was holding a sign reading, "Leffler." The Muktuk Kennels had sent over a cab to pick me up. When I got outside, I saw it was not just any cab. It was a stretch limousine. My expectations for this experience immediately sky-rocketed. I began to picture the luxurious castle where I would be spending the next two weeks.

After a 45-minute drive, over some rough and challenging roads, we pulled up to a tiny cabin. I quickly realized maybe my accom-modations would be a little sparser than I had previously imag-ined. There were no other cabins visible, and it turned out to be a 10-minute walk from my accommodations to the main lodge.

With some trepidation, I entered my abode, and reality struck me right between the eyes. It was a small 15-foot x 20-foot room. To say it was rustic would be a compliment. It was sparsely decorated with a table and two chairs, a gas heater, a bed, and a gas lantern over the table. I looked around for the light switch but found nothing. They also seemed to have hidden the television.

I quickly discovered there was NO electricity. I looked around for the bathroom and maybe a sink to wash up. There was also no running water or plumbing. Those amenities were all up at the lodge.

My first night was a real learning experience. It was 3:00 in the morning when it hit me. No, please, you can't be serious. My bladder was screaming at me that it was bursting. The sky was black with no moon in sight. I had to get out of bed and quickly put on some clothes and boots. If there had been any light, I could have seen my breath inside the room. I didn't know how to light the fireplace.

The temperature inside and out was a balmy 20 below. I quickly jumped into my clothes, put on my headlamp, and walked outside. The one saving grace was I only had to go number one. It was rather scary standing there, urging my bladder to get to work, while thinking that at any moment, a wolf could jump out from the shadows and attack me. Needless to say, after that, I was cautious about not consuming liquids before bed to ensure I didn't have to "go" in the middle of the night ever again.

All of our meals were in the main cabin, along with the only indoor bathroom and showers. The ground rules were that we were only allowed to shower every third day. The main house had electricity provided by a generator that was run sparingly. This at least did give me a chance to charge the batteries of my movie camera and computer.

Along with myself, there were five other mushers in training during the two weeks I was there. There was one couple who traveled from Norway. The kennels were managed by ten young people who came from different countries all around the world. In exchange for working with the dogs, they were provided with free room and board.

I became very close friends with Graeme and his wife, Cara. Graeme drew the short straw and was assigned the task of teaching me how to mush. We spent many quality hours together, where he attempted to teach me the finer points of mushing. To say Graeme had extreme patience would be an understatement. I told him if he ever decided to become a school teacher, I would hire him instantly.

Although I was 30 years older than all the "kids" who worked there, they seemed to accept me. I was very fortunate to experience something the other mushers missed out on. They must have taken pity on this poor, old guy who was all by himself.

I was invited into their inner circle, and we spent many nights sitting on the floor in their communal cabin, wearing headlamps and drinking a few libations. While they may not have spoken perfect

English, I learned a lot about Austria, Germany, Japan, Australia, and various other parts of the world. The last thing I expected to find during this adventure was "family." If I had to experience pre-COVID self-isolation in the middle of nowhere, I lucked out with this bunch of characters.

Lowell in the Yukon, 2009

The Best Team Ever

I will never forget the feeling of elation the day that I was first introduced to my team of dogs. There were six dogs in total, and except for a few times when one of them would go into heat, I was with these same six dogs for the entire two weeks. I got to know these dogs very well; their likes, their dislikes, their idiosyncrasies, even when they were going to have a bowel movement.

You may wonder why it was critical to know when they might have a BM. It was imperative, primarily if it occurred while we were sledding. Anyone who has owned a dog knows that when they have to go, they squat on their haunches to do their business. When the sled is moving along, and one of the dogs attempts to squat, they get run over by the other dogs and the sled.

As a musher, I had to keep my eyes open to know where I was going. If a dog began to squat, I had to immediately jam on the brake to stop the sled. It generally only took a matter of seconds, and we were back on our way again. Talk about learning things I would never have thought about.

Let me introduce my team in the picture below. Being a teacher, it was inevitable that I would categorize each dog according to the types of students I used to teach in my junior high classes. It is intriguing how dog personalities are not that different from humans.

Casper – She was my lead dog. She is pictured at the front left, with a black face. In the classroom, she would be the "keener." The one who not only wanted to know precisely how many words long an assignment should be, but also if she could do more for bonus points. She would wait patiently for my command and then take charge and lead us to where I wanted us to go. She WAS my favourite.

Jack – He is on Casper's right, and the best way to describe him was the "class clown." He was always smiling and looking for a good time or a distraction. He needed someone like Casper to keep him in line. He was very bright but would not want the others to know that was the case.

Ginger – She is next in the line, and Ginger was a "Princess." She didn't like getting up in the morning. To put her booties on, I would have to manually lift her body. Once she got going, she was a perfectionist. Best pace dog on the team. Very moody and pretended to ignore praise but secretly craved it.

Namik – He is behind Ginger. Without question, he was the typical rebellious adolescent. He was always pulling his booties off. He was sneaky and only defied me when I wasn't looking. When he knew I was looking, he pretended to be a saint.

Loudn – He is behind Ginger on the right. He was the big loveable oaf who could best be described as a horse who barks. He didn't know his own strength, and there was not a mean bone in his body. His only shortcomings were a lack of interpersonal skills and social awkwardness. I could never get mad at him because he always meant well, even if he didn't always do exactly what he should.

Jojo – She is beside Loudn, on the left. She was your typical adolescent athlete. Not the brightest bulb on the tree but built for speed and power. She would be your star athlete who tended to struggle with academics. She was not afraid to sweat and very focused. Once she knew what needed to be done, she did it.

There are two more dogs in the picture below, but usually, there were just the six listed above.

No Such Thing as a Free Ride

After breakfast and the morning chores of cleaning the compound were completed, we did our training. Each day we would go on a run with our dogs. The runs would last 2-3 hours, and we usually ran up to 30 kilometers each day. We started training on the flat river and proceeded to the hills and trees, which required a lot more skill on the part of the musher.

One surprising thing I learned was that we never had to stop and water the dogs, along the way. As they were running along, they would quench their thirst by reaching down to grab a mouthful of snow. That was all they needed to stay hydrated.

Sometimes it was a little unnerving, training on the Tahkini River. While the River was frozen over and easily supported our weight, often we would come to a spot where there might be six inches of water we had to go through. When there is a heavy accumulation of snow on a River, the snow's weight pushes the ice down. This pressure squeezes the water out along the sides of the river, where it will flow back onto the ice into the low spots.

It was always a major inconvenience when you came to open water on top of the ice. The sled had to be stopped and flipped onto its side. This prevented the dogs from taking off when the musher climbed off the sled. I had to take all the dog's booties off before going through the water. If the booties got soaked, the dogs could get blisters.

After we got through the water, I put the booties back on again, so their paws didn't freeze or get injured from sharp ice. The dogs were always ready to run, and as soon as I flipped the sled back over and released the brake, they were off like a shot.

While Graeme, my instructor, taught me a lot about mushing, I also learned from the dogs. I remember the first time we started driving in the hills and were in the middle of climbing a long hill. I noticed the lead dogs would turn around and look at me. I had no idea what they were doing. Soon all of the dogs turned and looked at me, and then they completely stopped running.

There I was, standing on the sled and going nowhere with all the dogs turned around looking at me. As soon as I stepped off the sled, the dogs took off. Luckily, I was able to grab the sled and hop back on. As soon as I stepped back onto the sled, they all stopped running again.

This time, I held on to the sled and stepped off the runners. Once again, they took off, and I was left holding on and running behind the sled. They kept running until the moment I jumped back on the sled. It finally clicked on me. They were telling me that there is no "free" ride here. When you are going up a hill, get your fat butt off the sled and help push the sled up the incline. Once they had taught me that lesson, we never again had a problem going up hills.

This adventure taught me how to mush, but it also taught me how to be a better teacher and parent. When I say all parents should treat their kids like a dog, I mean they should:

1. Give them personal attention every day
2. Treat them fairly, not equally
3. Establish routines and be firm, not cruel
4. Train them to be leaders
5. Know the strengths and weaknesses of each
6. Nourish them with positive encouragement

I would argue that most successful parents and teachers do these things instinctively.

Never Step on a Cross

Our two-week mushing adventure culminated with our graduation exercises. These included a three-day, two-night camp out in a tent. If we survived, we passed the course and could proudly proclaim ourselves to be mushers extraordinaire. The very cool part of this was that we ran the same trail the Yukon Quest racers had used several days before. We did not make it the entire 1000 miles that the Quest racers endured. We only completed about half of the first leg of their journey, roughly 80 kilometers.

With the weather turning bitterly cold, we ended up with only three mushers participating in the final adventure. The other two mushers could only stay one night, so it was just Graeme, me, the dogs, and the great outdoors after they left.

The first thing you learn about mushing is that the dogs always come first. Whenever we stopped for a rest or to eat, we went through the same routine. First, we had to start a fire to melt snow and get water to make the dogs their food and provide something for us to drink. While the snow was melting, we had to take the harness off each dog and tie them far enough apart so they couldn't fight. It is another example of how much teenagers and dogs are alike.

Once we had the water, we mixed in frozen kibbles and chicken parts with high-fat content. This gave the dogs the energy to run in the extreme cold. We never had to "try" to get the dogs to eat. Usually, the food was gone before the bowls hit the ground.

Next up, it was our turn to eat. You might think we would be roughing it—Au contraire. Graeme was a fantastic cook. His nickname was Dutch Oven because he used only a dutch oven to prepare a delectable spread of meat, potatoes, and vegetables. He could even use a dutch oven for baking a cake over an open fire.

For the overnight, we stopped at a place where bales had been previously placed. The straw was strewn where the dogs would sleep, giving them a warm bed to lie on.

To get our sleeping accommodations ready, we had to shovel the snow away from an area big enough for us to pitch the tent. Since it usually got dark around 4:00 pm, after we ate and sat around the fire for a bit, it was early to bed. Before we bedded down, we had to check the dogs' feet for cuts or bruises and put on a salve that kept their feet supple. This salve was in a tin can that we slept with under our shirts, next to our skin. The reason was that it was impossible to use when it was frozen into a block of ice.

I talked earlier about the professional mushers who ran the Quest race starting the trip with 14 dogs, not six like we had. The negative thing about having that many dogs is by the time you melt the snow for water, feed the dogs, and check their feet, you might have a couple of hours for yourself to try to sleep. Over ten or more days of racing, the biggest problem a racer can face is falling asleep on the sled and falling off. The dogs will just keep on running. To avoid this problem, the mushers strap themselves to the sled to prevent them from falling off if they do fall asleep.

If there was a problem with one of the dogs, they can't just leave them. The injured dog was placed on the sled, where they were carried to the next checkpoint and dropped off. The racer must have at least five dogs left to finish the race.

The first night of our stay in the tent was a little crisp. With it being 30 below outside and the same inside the tent, we decided to use a small propane heater to keep us warm. We soon realized that the sleeping bags we had were so well insulated that we didn't need the heater. So, once we settled in, we shut the heater off. When you first got undressed and jumped into the ice-cold bag, it was a bit of a shock. However, once you zipped the bag up, so there was nothing more than your nose sticking out, it quickly became quite comfortable.

Falling asleep after a long day of mushing was pretty easy. Until the dreaded time when your aging body tells you, "it's time for a pee." This involved using your headlamp to find your frozen clothes to put on while your teeth chattered loud enough to wake everyone else up. Once you were fully dressed, you had to stumble over everyone between you and the tent opening to make your exit.

After exiting the tent, I will never forget looking at the dogs and seeing many eyes staring back. Most dogs' eyes shine yellow when you hit them with light. Huskies are different. Their eyes glowed a bright red, reminding me of a horror movie with the devil as the leading actor.

Getting back to the title of this story, I would be remiss if I didn't tell you about how we started training for the toilet paper shortage of 2020. Long before COVID-19 was in the news, we learned how to conserve TP. Without getting into too much detail, the most important thing was not to pollute. We had to carefully measure out toilet paper squares that we took with us, along with a brown paper bag. The funniest description I have heard about TP conservation is that before COVID-19, I spun the roll like it was the Wheel of Fortune, and after, it was more like I was cracking a safe.

Once we had finished our business, the soiled paper was placed into the paper bag and carried back to camp, where we burned it in the campfire. And to ensure we did not step in anyone else's jobs, we made a cross of two sticks and put it over the snow we had covered the evidence with. When you went out in the middle of the night, the most important thing was not to step on any crosses.

This next day was the first time Graeme trusted me enough to let me go alone, on my own, with the dogs. Generally, we were never out of his sight for more than a couple of minutes. This time, he let me go off on my own, and it was over an hour before I saw him again. The beauty of the surroundings, along with the sounds of crunching snow below the sled and dogs panting, made this the most memorable part of the trip.

Casper, My Friendly Ghost

The two weeks of mushing went by far too quickly. Soon, it was the last night of my adventure. Whenever I do something, I always try to live the most complete experience possible. If you are going to do something, you might just as well do it the best you can.

Some of the paid guests were satisfied with limiting their experience to when they "ran" the dogs and were mushing. I quickly discovered it was a lot of work to take care of 125 dogs, and the more hands that could help made for less work.

I would get up early to help mix 125 breakfasts each day. This involved breaking apart frozen chicken parts and combining them with warm water to form a high-energy stew. We then took the bowls out to distribute to each of the dogs.

Once breakfast was finished, it was time to clean up. We had shovels and pans we used to scoop the poop that had been deposited all around the dog houses. The cold weather was a blessing because it is much easier to scoop frozen excrement.

After the scooping was completed, it was our turn for breakfast. This process was repeated for lunch and supper, so there was always something to do. In between, we did our training, as well as help when day visitors would come for a ride. I enjoyed working with the tourists because they treated us like expert dog handlers who knew everything there was to know about mushing.

Sometimes, there was the occasional problem we had to deal with. In preparation for a quick tourist trip, we would hitch the dogs up to the sled and tie it to a post until they were ready to run. On one occasion, I helped a young newlywed couple from Japan who did not speak any English. The first thing I would do is explain that you do NOT untie the sled until you are ready to go. This time, I forgot to mention that fact. I helped the young lady sit in the sled and showed the husband how to stand on the runners at the back of the sleigh. As I was going to the front of the dogs to check their harnesses, the young man decided to untie the sled.

As soon as the dogs felt the release of the restraint, they took off at full speed ahead. Immediately, the man flipped off the back of the sled and left the young lady, screaming as the dogs bolted off. Luckily, I was able to lunge forward and grab the harness of one of the dogs. They did not drag me too far before I could get them stopped and help pacify the terrified guest.

On the last night in my cabin, I decided it would be nice to have a little company. I asked Frank if Casper could sleep in the room with me. Casper was my lead dog, and she was the one I had become most attached to. Frank said it would be fine, but since Casper had never slept inside, I probably wouldn't get too much sleep. I assumed she would curl up on the throw rug beside my bed. As soon as I crawled under the covers, she jumped up and curled her body inside my arm. This was where she was when I fell asleep and when I awoke in the morning.

All too soon, my adventure was over, and I was saying goodbye to my newfound family and also to the humans I had gotten to know. Muktuk has a tradition where, if you are interested, they will put your name on the list for one of the dogs. When that dog retires and is too old to sled anymore, they will call you. If you are still interested, you can take the dog home to live out the rest of its life with you. Luckily, Casper had not been promised to anyone, so I gave them my phone number and told them to call me when she retired.

It was about five years later that I got an email from Graeme indicating that Casper was available and was mine if I still wanted her. By then, we had started spending our winters in Arizona, and I didn't think a northern dog would appreciate the desert life and heat down south. I had to grudgingly decline. Timing is everything, and sometimes it sucks.

A Fish Story

For every great angler, there is a better liar. Maybe liar might be a little harsh, so let's be kind and call them creative storytellers. If there were any truth about the "big" ones that got away, the lakes and streams would be full of creatures like Ogopogo and the Lochness Monster. While I sometimes may exaggerate, I do have my share of "stories," and I guarantee there is at least some degree of truth associated with each.

For more summers than I can remember, we spent several weeks each year fishing the lakes and streams of South-Eastern British Columbia. Usually, this was in and around the Cranbrook area. While the fish in streams seldom get to be very large, if you are lucky enough to hit a hungry "school," you can catch more than you can keep. The majority of the time was spent fishing the streams close to where we were camped. For some variety, we would take a road trip once in a while.

The one central tenet of fishing is that the easier it is to get to a location, the more anglers there will be and the fewer fish available to catch. With all the off-road vehicles these days, there are very few places left that would be considered "virgin territory." Forty years ago, we only had our half-ton trucks and feet to get us to our destination. This sounds very similar to the story about walking to school, five miles, uphill both ways, through quicksand and driving blizzards. Occasionally, we did manage to find a lake that made the long journey well worth the effort.

It was during one scouting trip, after a good deal of bushwhacking with our old truck and then a long hike, that we arrived at a destination that looked like it had been plucked out of a Hans Christian Anderson fable. The water was crystal clear, and when you cast your bait out, you could see several fish rush towards it. You could be selective and pull the hook away if the fish was too small. It was one of those times you only dream about, where you had fish biting with every cast you made. We were just there for a few hours, but during that time, we each pulled in close to a hundred fish. It "almost" got to be a little boring.

One of the reasons the fishing was so good was that very few people had fished there. The way we know that to be true was because on that first trip, my sister had left her creel behind. When we returned to the lake a couple of years later, there was her creel with all the hooks and her fishing license still sitting in the same spot she had left it.

My dad often told his story about the biggest fish he ever caught. He was fishing from shore at the Forks, north of Grassy Lake. He hooked a monster that ended up taking him a few hours to land. Non-fisher types don't realize it, but there are sturgeon that bottom feed in our southern rivers. These fish can grow up to several hundred pounds in weight. While my dad struggled to reel this fish in, he ended up with an audience, alongside him on the shore, cheering on his efforts. One of these spectators wore a uniform and worked for the Department of Fish and Wildlife. Since Dad did not have a special license to keep a sturgeon, the Wildlife officer tagged the fish before it was released so it could be monitored at a later date.

The best fish story I can personally relate to happened during one of the summer trips our family would take in our truck and camper. On this most memorable of trips, we were traveling to Jasper. Several things happened on this trip that I can remember. The first occurred when we attempted to climb a fairly steep hill leading up to the Athabasca Ice Fields. As we were slowly crawling along, the truck finally gave up the ghost and stalled. It was a very narrow road. Rather than block the traffic, we had to slowly back down until we reached a turn-off, where we could be towed to a service station.

The fix was nothing significant, and although we never reached the Ice Fields, we did end up stopping at a place with the exotic name of Honeymoon Lake. We checked it out and discovered you could rent a small fishing boat. We were told there were some colossal trout just waiting to be caught. I remember waking up the next morning to go fishing and looking at the bucket of water that had been left out. It was frozen solid. No wonder we had to turn the heater on in the middle of the night.

The first day of fishing was pretty successful as we brought in a full string of trout, each around a couple of pounds. I can remember proudly carrying this haul back to our camper and stopping for congratulations while other vacationers looked on with envy. The next day was even better. Within the first hour of morning fishing, we caught three beauties, with one almost four pounds in size.

I will never forget when we caught the fourth fish. To keep the fish alive and fresh, we used a stringer chain attached to the boat. The chain could hold up to eight fish by stringing each on a separate hook. Once they were on the chain, they would float in the water alongside the boat. I unhooked the chain from the boat, so I could lift the entire string to admire our catch. When one of the fish, close to my hand, started flopping around, I jumped back and let go of the chain.

I remember seeing the chain, full of fish, sinking into the water and out of sight. My father was not a man of many words, but I remember learning a few "new" ones that day. When we went in for lunch, there were no smiles on either of our faces.

We did go back out in the afternoon, but the fish had stopped biting. We ended up getting skunked, which is another name for no fish on board. The great thing about having a boat is that you have some fishing options. You either anchor in one spot and cast out, or you can trawl, leaving the lines out behind you. As we were on our way in, we had left the lines out until we reached the shore.

Suddenly, Dad got a strike on his line. It had to be a big one because the line bent straight down towards the water. As he reeled it in, we couldn't wait to see the trophy attached to the other end. When we were finally able to see the catch, it was NOT a big one. It was the four fish I had lost earlier that morning. Dad's hook had snagged the group that had been floating around all that time.

While my dad is no longer around to serve as my witness, that is *Our Fish Story,* and I am sticking to it.

Strange Things Done
Under the Midnight Sun

In the late 1980s, a motley group of over-the-hill ballplayers formed the *Foremost Prime Time* slow-pitch team. Even though Foremost has a population base of approximately only 800 people, we were able to field some outstanding talent on this team.

I played rover in the outfield, and my greatest strength was out-running hits and diving to catch the ball before it hit the ground. All those dives and collisions with the earth have come back to haunt me in my older years. The aches and pains remind me daily of the way I badly mistreated my body.

For several years, we were pretty successful in many tournaments around the area and decided it was time to determine whether we were as good as we thought we were. In 1991, we entered our first provincial qualifier in Calgary and played well, winning the right to represent Alberta at the Yukon nationals.

We decided, along with our close friends, the Magnesons, to make a trip out of it by driving to the Yukon in their motorhome. Glen and Jay, along with their sons, Brent and Cody, became the traveling partners of Irene and me, along with our son Dusty. We left our daughters Andrea and Courtney with my parents, as there was not enough room in the motorhome for all of us.

It was a close encounter of the first kind, as the three boys slept in the space above the cab. Glen and Jay slept in the bed that also served as our table, while Irene and I slept at the back on the seats that pulled out. Considering the proximity that we shared for a couple of weeks, we had many more good memories than the other kind. The trip up took several days, and we made sure we could enjoy the journey along with the destination.

One of the most memorable places we stopped at was the Liard Hot Springs, located close to the town of *100-mile House*. It was basically in the middle of nowhere. This phenomenon was unspoiled and existed in its natural state. There was no one taking admission, no paved sidewalks, and you swam at your own risk. It was not unusual to find bears in the area. While we never spotted any bears, this area indeed was an oasis in the middle of the desert.

To this day, everyone still fondly remembers sitting in the stream and basking in the natural heat of the water. Not far from these hot springs, we stopped at a small service station to gas up. The only thing I remember about this was that we were given a felt pen and told to sign our name somewhere. It was no easy feat as there were names on the wall, the floor, and even the ceilings. Finding an open spot took some searching, but we did manage to leave our markings for all of eternity.

A day later, we found a lake that looked like it could be a great fishing spot. I don't remember if we caught any fish, but I remember Brent snagging Glen. Brent's backswing came too close during one of his casts, and the hook caught Glen in the thigh. Several of us played *doctor* before we were finally able to extract the hook from Glen's leg. I think that was the end of fishing for the rest of the trip.

After several days of driving, we eventually met up with the rest of the team, who had chosen to fly. The most memorable thing about the tournament was that it didn't get dark until well past midnight. We were able to practice until the wee hours of the morning. Of course, we didn't practice all night because we had to celebrate a little, as well.

Dusty and the Magneson boys had a great time during the tournament. We had taken a multitude of Foremost pins that they traded for pins from other provinces. They ended up with at least a hundred different pins from across Canada. After each game, they would also make a trip around the ball diamonds to retrieve the balls that had been hit as home runs over the outfield fence. They found enough balls to keep our team well-stocked for a few years, and there were even extras they managed to sell back to the tournament organizers for 50 cents a ball.

We ended up finishing fifth overall in the tournament. We were not used to playing against such a high caliber of ball where most of the players on the other teams were homerun hitters. We only had a couple of big hitters, with the rest of us happy to find open holes anywhere in the outfield.

I will never forget the horrible start to my hitting. In the first game, I went hitless, going 0 for 4. In the next match, I went 0 for 3 before being yanked for another player. That was the first time I remember getting pulled out of a game because of bad play. While I deserved this, I can remember thinking that this will NOT happen again. Lucky for me, I did get to start the next game and the rest of the games after that. I did not realize it at the time, but I ended up hitting 14 of 14 for the remainder of the tournament.

I will never forget sitting in the stands at the end of the tournament while the awards were given to the winning team and the all-stars. It was no surprise when they announced Nyle, from our team, as an all-star infielder because of his usual exceptional defense at shortstop and the many home runs he hit for us.

What they announced next was a complete and utter shock. I can remember the announcer saying, "and the next all-star outfielder is .... Lowell Leffler". Our entire team was dumbfounded, none more so than me. Walking onto the field to receive the all-star plaque was as surreal as a dream. It was so unbelievable that to this day, I don't think I remember much of anything about it. I do have the plaque, however, so it must have happened. And while I played pretty well in the outfield, it was my going 14/14 in the last four games and finishing with a 667-batting average overall that cinched it. I bet I was the only all-star there who has never hit a home run in his entire life.

We Are the Champions

As I stated in my last story, we had been very successful the previous year, when we won the Alberta title, which qualified us for nationals in Whitehorse, Yukon. The next year, 1992, we played even better, winning virtually every tournament, both old-timers and open. When we beat all competition at provincials, we once again qualified for nationals.

This time we did not have to drive far, as the nationals were hosted in Calgary. We were very familiar with the diamonds located near the Cross Roads Hotel, as we had played in many tournaments at the same complex. Many of us would bring up our trailers or RVs and park on the grounds. They used to leave one of the gates open for us at night to access the public washrooms.

We had a very successful round-robin, winning our way into the playoffs. We were not the strongest team, and we did not hit the most home runs. However, we were flawless in the field and managed to hit enough seeing-eye singles, to come out with victories.

The most memorable game of the tournament was the final game, which we played against Ontario. They were an awesome collection of home run hitters who had no problem pounding the ball over the fence, almost every time at-bat. Our team had only a couple of legitimate long ball hitters, those being Nyle and Ken.

In the final game, we lucked out with the weather. The field we played on faced directly into a fierce wind blowing into home plate.

This was the best advantage we could have hoped for because it killed their long balls while it did not affect our line drives. Whenever they would blast one up into the air, the wind held it short of the fence so we could run under and catch the flyball. It ended up being a very low-scoring game.

We took turns coaching when our runners were on base. It was getting to be late in the game when I was coaching third base, and we had a runner on second. Someone hit the ball to the right field for a single. I remember our runner from second coming towards third. Because the game was tied and runs were at a premium, I wanted so badly for us to score on this hit. I waved the runner around third and towards home. When the outfielder threw a perfect strike to home plate, the catcher was able to tag our runner out. My heart sank, and I can remember thinking I screwed up and it probably cost us everything.

Believe it or not, my opportunity to make up for the previous mistake was presented to me only minutes later. It was the bottom of the ninth inning, and the score was tied 1-1. There were runners on third and first and two out. The next batter up was me. I remember taking a couple of pitches without swinging. The next pitch was the one I was looking for. I swung the bat as hard as I could and made solid contact.

I took off running, as fast as my feet would fly, for first base. We all watched the ball as if we were observing it in slow motion. The ball was a low, climbing drive towards the shortstop. I can remember the shortstop jumping into the air while the ball was slowly rising in front of him. It reminded me of an airplane trying to take off in a field where the trees are quickly approaching, and you are not sure if it will actually clear the top of the trees.

I saw the shortstop stretch from a perfectly timed jump and watched as the ball glanced off the top of his glove. The ball dropped to the ground behind him, and I crossed the first base bag safely. This managed to score the winning run from third base. As soon as I touched first base, Nyle, who was already running towards me, grabbed me in a bear hug and raised me in the air. How many times in a person's life do you get to score the winning run in a national championship where your team is crowned the "best" in all of Canada? It definitely goes down as one of the most memorable moments of my life.

Lowell, pictured in the front row, second from the right with the National Champion Foremost Prime Time Slow Pitch Team

Work-Related

Can Lightning Strike Twice

No job I have ever held has had the excitement and danger of diffusing bombs or welding underwater at 300 feet below the ocean's surface. At some point in our lives, I am sure we all have been tempted to look for shortcuts to make our jobs easier. Sometimes this has accidentally resulted in the job becoming potentially harmful to our health and well-being. Also, there are often occasions when we look to scare or prank someone, and the result is a little more severe than we had anticipated.

An example of something that did not have life-threatening consequences, but did not seem funny at the time, occurred when I worked for the Town of Bow Island. We were responsible for getting the Bert Knibbs Ball Park ready for the season. There were rocks to pick, grass to cut, and weeds to whip. Often, we were charged with getting rid of insect homes that presented possible dangers for the public and players. One such incident involved a gigantic nest of red ants. We determined that the best way to deal with this was to burn them out.

While we were waiting for someone to run to the mower and bring back some gas, a fellow worker, who shall remain nameless, and I were leaning on our shovels waiting. I didn't think much of it when he decided to put his shovel into the nest and take out a full scoop of dirt and ants. When he threw the load at me and covered me in ants, I quickly reacted. Those little critters pack a nasty bite, and all I could think of was how fast I could get my clothes off. I have never got undressed that fast ever again. Other than a few bites, I was not harmed, but I was more than a little ticked off. While I don't remember specifically, I am sure there was some retaliation involved later.

Another summer, I worked for New West Homes in Calgary. Our primary responsibility was building fences after the new homes had been constructed. These fences were all wood, with 1-inch x 6-inch planks nailed onto 4-inch x 4-inch posts anchored in the ground. The first thing we had to do was dig the fence post holes before securing the post by tamping and reinforcing it with dirt. This was a lot of work and seemed to take forever.

At one of our job sites, a caterpillar worked in the next yard. The operator was also employed by New West, and we would have coffee with him during our breaks. I asked if he would be interested in trying out a little experiment. It occurred to me that if he would fill his bucket with dirt, there might be a quick way to get the fence posts into the ground. He said he would give it a go.

My job was to hold the fence post while he centered the bucket over the post and then pushed it down into the ground. I remember the first few posts going in like butter. We were sure we could finish the job quickly and then have some free time to do whatever we wanted. It was about the fourth post in that we hit some hard ground. While I was holding the post, it was not going down, and then all of a sudden, the post snapped. When that happened, the bucket dropped and came within inches of my head. I didn't need the Workers Compensation Board to tell me this was not the safest way to build fences, and we were soon back to digging the holes by hand. Definitely, NOT the smartest thing I have ever done.

Aside from building fences, we also planted trees in the front yard of each new home built. The trees were delivered in the back of a 3-ton truck. One of us would work up in the box, handing down trees to the other workers who would take them to be planted. When

I call them trees, you have to realize they were only about five feet tall and not very heavy. More like big twigs.

One day, I was in the back of the truck, and the weather was very overcast. It was drizzling slightly, and there was some lightning activity around us. I remember lifting one of the trees over the side of the box and hearing a buzz as I held it up. I saw a flash of light, and I felt a shock run down my arm. It knocked me on my butt, but thanks to the truck's tires, I was grounded, and it didn't do any damage. I am not saying this was a direct lightning blast, but there was enough electricity to get my heart racing.

The other time I had an encounter with lightning was on a plane flying into London, England. We were starting our descent to the airport and going through a rain cloud. I remember seeing a flash on the wing across the aisle and hearing a boom. It scared the crap out of all of us in that section. Further back in the plane, no one even knew what had happened.

It is not uncommon for this to happen as commercial jet airliners in the US are struck by lightning once every 1,000 flight hours or once each year, on average. The lightning typically strikes a relatively sharp edge of a plane, like a wingtip or a nose, and the current exits via the tail. Again, no grounding, no damage. This goes to show you that it is always best to be "well-grounded" in life.

Education, A Life Sentence

I have always told others that I was one of the only people in the world, who spent his entire life in school. Seriously, it started several days after I was born. My mother was a teacher in a small, isolated one-room schoolhouse, teaching students of all ages and grades. Back then, paid maternity leave had not yet been invented.

Several days after giving birth, my mother was back in the classroom. Not having any other option, she took me to school, where I spent the majority of the day sleeping in my bassinet at the back of the room. No, I wasn't put in the corner because of bad behaviour. That didn't happen until the teachers started expecting me to sit still at a desk and learn.

Since there were older students in the classroom, Mom incorporated me into their home economics lesson. It involved their going to the back if I started to cry, to distract, and quiet me. Generally, the problem was that I was hungry. I am confident that the students did not complain about a few extra recesses while my mother fed me.

When I did start school, it was in Grassy Lake, and the most excruciating year of my life was Grade 2. I was in trouble, day and night. My mother was the teacher, and the principal was my Uncle Nick. If I got into trouble at school, my mother knew about it immediately, and the punishment and lectures continued even after I arrived home.

I remember spending many, many recesses in the school basement typing room, watching the high school students in typing class. The typing room had windows to peek in to see the students below. We thought it was fun to make faces through the windows and distract the typing class. You'll never guess who the teacher was. Of course, it was Uncle Nick, the principal. He would sneak out and catch us red-handed and make us come down and sit quietly until the recess bell rang. To this day, I feel this was one of the main reasons I have well-developed skills on the keyboard.

The greatest desire of all teachers is to look back on their career and feel they have made a positive impact on the students that went through their classes. I believe after having taught hundreds of different students, that I may have taught at least one of them something. Several of my ex-students from the St. Margaret days in Calgary are friends here on Facebook and may end up reading this. They turned out to be pretty terrific adults, despite me.

I will never forget, however, an incident that occurred years after I had left the classroom to get involved in Administration. I was at a Summer Conference in Waterton, and we had a presenter who was introducing us to the new and wonderful world of "Smartboards." It was after the presentation when, not the presenter, but her husband came over and spoke to me. He began with, "You probably don't remember me, but I was in the first class you taught in Calgary." That would have been approximately 20 years earlier, and he was right; I didn't remember him.

As I said earlier, over the years, we meet hundreds of students, and unfortunately, the ones you generally remember are the students who gave you the most grief. This student was not one of those, but he was in the class that the teachers had nicknamed the "sweat hogs." They were reminiscent of the old television show "Welcome Back Cotter."

I listened as he shared a couple of stories that he thought might help me remember him. All of a sudden, out of nowhere, he told me, point-blank, "The thing I remember most about you is how mean you were and how scared I was of you." Isn't that a legacy every teacher hopes to leave behind? I was speechless and didn't know what to say. After several seconds of silence, he rescued me by moving on to another topic, and after chatting for a while, we went our separate ways. I was mortified and in shock and denial.

To give you some background, I need to explain the circumstances a little more thoroughly. I graduated from university when I was 22, and my first job was at St. Margaret's Junior High School in Calgary. I was teaching Jr. High science, so some of my students were only seven years younger than me, and many of them were "bigger."

I had graduated at Christmas time, and it was in the 1970s when teaching positions were plentiful. I attended an interview with the principal and vice-principal and was hired on the spot. The only thing I remember about the interview was being told I would be the fifth teacher for their classroom since September. I swear to God, the principal told me that he didn't care what I taught them, as long as I kept them in the room and quiet.

The school was involved in a new teaching philosophy where they divided the students up homogeneously, depending on ability and work ethic. The Grade nine students were divided into three different groupings. The top class had 41 students in it, but they were all keeners and hard workers. Next, there was an intermediate class of 30 students. Finally, there were the 18 sweat hogs remaining to be lumped together. They were identified as underachievers and were grouped with others who did not care about learning. Talk about a recipe for disaster.

You can easily guess which of these classes was the most challenging. Remember that four teachers had left before my arrival, for a variety of reasons, none of them positive. I did adopt a tough persona with the sole intent of maintaining order and decorum. This was for self-preservation. Even though it was still legal to strap students, there was nothing I could have done physically to change any of their behaviour. I had a pretty good idea that some of them may have lived on the street, at least part-time.

Long story short, I did start as a Gestapo agent, but by the end of the year, I had developed some good relationships with many of the students, even some of the sweat hogs. I never did have to resort to any of those military tactics in future years. Unfortunately, that one student was in the class, not so much for his behaviour but more for his lack of motivation and learning ability. I was so preoccupied with "dealing with the most obvious problems" that I didn't spend enough time getting to know him and others like him who were not the "trouble makers."

I would give myself a failing grade as a beginning teacher, but over time, I learned what it meant to be a good teacher. The most valuable lesson that applies not only to teaching, but life in general is ….NO ONE CARES HOW MUCH YOU KNOW UNTIL THEY KNOW HOW MUCH YOU CARE!

I Could Have Been a Mortician

In high school, I was not the most academically focused student. I had not ever thought about life after Grade 12 and had absolutely no career plans for the future. My biggest concern was whether or not there was life after the weekend. I cannot remember my parents ever telling me they expected me to go to university. It was an unstated given, and there was never any doubt about it.

That is until I realized you had to have a certain grade point average if you were hoping to be accepted into university. At the time, the universities expected you to have a 65% GPA. Fortunately for me, there must not have been the expected number of students apply, so my less than stellar 57% was enough to get me in.

In Grade 11, our Vice Principal, Mr. Roth, did administer an aptitude test to me. It was designed to summarize my strengths and skills and make suggestions for future jobs I might do well at. When we met to discuss the results, I remember him stating it looks like I would make a great mortician.

I am not sure if it was my personality or ability, or lack thereof, to get along with people that moved me in that direction. He made a couple of jokes about how "people were dying to get in to see the mortician" and how "a mortician never ran out of customers." At first, I thought he was kidding, but then I realized he was *dead* serious. While I never considered working with the "stone-cold," I am sure many of my students would argue that I may have bored many of them to death.

In university, I quickly realized the professors could care less if you attended their class or not. They also utilized this utterly unfair way of evaluating students. It involved you turning in labs and assignments regularly. Once I learned you couldn't pass just by doing well on the final exam, my study habits greatly improved.

I started university thinking I might become a pharmacist, but I decided to switch to education when I realized how many years it would take. In the seventies, there was an extreme shortage of teachers in Alberta. I can remember having one year left before I graduated and having the Calgary education system visit us at the university. They were prepared to offer me a position if I would sign an agreement, then and there. We didn't even need to complete our last year of schooling. I was not sure I wanted to stay in a big city, so I decided to wait and take my chances after the completion of my degree.

It is mind-boggling to realize how much things have changed in terms of what we could and couldn't do in the classroom. The strap was a common form of discipline, although it could only be used on the palms of the hands. I remember my first principal expecting us to use the strap as a deterrent. The new teachers would hold practice sessions, using each other as guinea pigs. We didn't want to look inept if we had to punish someone with the strap. This seems almost unbelievable, but back then, even the parents expected us to use corporal punishment.

As a science teacher, I routinely had my students do labs that today are entirely unacceptable. As part of my Grade 7 unit on genetics, every student was involved in blood typing. The students would typically prick each other's fingers with a lancet and put drops of blood on a microscope slide. They would add two different antigens to the slide and look for clumping or clotting. It was easy to determine which of the four blood types they were. If there was no clotting, their blood was type O, and they were the universal donors.

Generally, the process went well once all the drama about stabbing themselves subsided. Occasionally, we did have a student pass out during the lab. It was generally the biggest and toughest boy, and other than some good-natured teasing from the girls, we never had an issue.

I am sure you wonder what the parents said when I contacted them about their son passing out. It never occurred to me to call them, and I'm pretty sure the students involved never let them know either. Sometimes, it would come up at a parent-teacher conference, and we would all have a good laugh about it. It was no big deal; it was just the way things were done at the time.

Another lab that we did was a student favourite because of the noise it made. The students would run an electric current through water and use inverted test tubes to collect the released gases. The students learned that when water is decomposed, the resultant by-products are oxygen and hydrogen. Once we had gathered the two gases, it was time to test them.

To test for oxygen, a wooden match was lit and then blown out. By immediately inserting the match into the upside-down test tube, the oxygen would cause it to reignite and flare-up. The hydrogen test involved holding a lit match at the bottom of the tube.

In case you don't know, hydrogen gas is the lightest element. That was why it was used in the Hindenburg Dirigible in 1937. Unfortunately, there was a side effect that had dire consequences. When the students would hold the match under the hydrogen tube, they only had to get it "close" before it would explode and make a loud booming sound. It was always the most fun to observe the first group that did the test because they were invariably shocked at how loud the bang was. And I had forgotten to tell them what to expect. Whoops.

While you may think these two lab experiments were somewhat dangerous procedures to involve students, I must tell you about a lab back in the sixties that was part of the science curriculum. It involved the mixing of hydrochloric acid and sodium hydroxide. Hydrochloric acid was the main component in car batteries. It is strongly acidic and could severely burn the skin on contact. Sodium hydroxide is a very corrosive "base" and can burn skin and melt your hair. The chemical reaction looked like this:

$NaOH + HCl = H2O + NaCl$

When these toxic substances were mixed, the product formed was water and salt. The students could actually taste the salt water, and as long as they had titrated everything in the correct amounts, there was no problem. It doesn't take a rocket surgeon to imagine the possible pitfalls that may have occurred if the students were not accurate enough in their titrations.

While I don't remember any newsworthy accidents ever happening in laboratories across the province, I cringe now, even thinking about some of the things we routinely used to do in the name of experimentation.

All I Want for Christmas Is ...

My favourite classes at university were related to the field of zoology. I found the study of animals much more interesting than learning about plants and photosynthesis.

I have to admit that we sometimes performed experiments with specific plants such as cannabis Sativa. Of course, this was purely for scientific research and the desire to expand our horizons in the field of academia. Proof once again, we were a generation ahead of their time. We figured out the many medicinal benefits of marijuana way back in 1972. It took the Canadian government 46 years to come to the same conclusion on October 17, 2018, when it was finally legalized.

Animal dissection was the emphasis of most of our zoology classes. One of the first creatures of my dissecting career was a dog shark. During the first class, we received a 4-foot shark that we would become intimate with over the next several weeks. Having gutted and cleaned hundreds of fish over the years, I felt confident that this was right up my alley.

I quickly learned that speed was not the factor I was being graded upon. For some reason, the professor wanted us to spend all our time with the things I used to rip out and throw away. I was expected to carefully search through the entrails and identify, catalog, and classify all major organs. After each lab, we wrapped our fish up and put it in cold storage until the following week.

Even though they had been preserved in formaldehyde, after a few weeks, they began to take on an "aire" of their own. By the time we completed our studies on them, they stank to high heaven. It so happened that the timing was excellent, and the end of our dissection corresponded with a university tradition called "Bermuda Shorts Day."

Everyone dressed up for the beach and water activities, especially in the residences where water ran everywhere. It was the perfect scenario for us to take our rotting shark cadavers to chase the female students around the science theatres. Somehow in our warped minds, we thought this would be a great way to meet women.

The next part of the class involved our working with vertebrates. We never did any work on human cadavers, and to be honest, I doubt I would have been able to do that. I had watched far too many Boris Karloff movies to know that dead bodies can spring back to life at any time. I didn't think the little scalpel I was holding was going to do anything to re-kill a zombie that I had somehow ticked off by cutting into them.

Fortunately for me, I have always been a dog person, so when I realized we would be dissecting a cat, I did not have to worry about any emotional attachments getting in the way. I named my kitty Stiffy because of the resulting rigor mortis. I found the cat much more interesting than working on a fish because the cat's body systems are much more similar to our own. After several weeks of intimacy with Stiffy, I did develop a new respect for cats. It affected me to such a degree that I decided to boycott all eating establishments rumored to use felines for their sweet and sour ribs.

The dissection activity I found the most disturbing involved the use of frogs. I have never personally had a pet frog, but this was the first time we cut something open that was still living. The first thing we had to do was "pith" the frog. To immobilize the frog, we stuck a pin through its brain, resulting in paralysis. We cut open the abdomen and exposed the heart.

The first time I observed a live, beating heart was a little traumatic. We would place a drop of chemical on the heart that would cause it to start beating rapidly. This was followed by another chemical to slow it down. We attached a wire to a graphing pen and recorded the heart's beating on paper. I realized after this lab that I was not "cut" out to be a doctor. By the end of the lab, I had "lost" my patient, and even though it was only a frog, I knew this type of work was not for me.

As a science teacher, I enjoyed teaching biology 30 the most. It involved the study of human physiology and reproduction. Living in Foremost and having friends who worked with cattle, I obtained all the organs I needed in my classroom. They would provide me with hearts, kidneys, brains, and lungs. Most of these organs were larger than human organs, so it was easy to observe and explore the various parts. Sometimes, the students taught me things. My classroom was separate from the lab, but it was right next door.

One day we were looking at and discussing the function of the lungs. I had a gigantic set of cow lungs on the table. I had to go to the classroom for a second to get something. Suddenly, there was a loud commotion from the lab. When I ran back to see what was happening, I couldn't believe my eyes. I found a student putting his hands and face over the trachea and blowing air into the lungs.

It was amazing to observe the size as they expanded and contracted with each breath. I had never seen this, in person and I was as shocked as the students were. I had never thought of having someone blow into the lungs, and I sure as heck wasn't going to do it myself.

The funniest memory I have of dissection in the classroom involved my Grade eight students from the St. Martha School. We studied the form and function of movement, and I had brought in chicken wings for the students to carefully examine and dissect. They could see how bones worked together with ligaments and tendons and extrapolate how this occurred in our bodies.

Unfortunately, we ran out of time, and the students did not finish the project. The plan was to take all the pans with the chicken parts, place them in the fridge and continue after the weekend. You have to realize that at 3:30, on the last day before a long weekend, the thoughts of the kids and the teacher have already moved on to what exciting things we would be doing over the holiday.

Somehow, through an oversight on my part, the wings were left out for the next three days and provided a huge surprise for me upon my return on Tuesday morning. I can remember turning the key to my room and opening the door. I was immediately hit between the eyes with the most disgusting smell I have ever encountered. The odors were so foul that even after opening every window in the room, the stench was unbearable. I had to hold all my classes for the day in the gym. I was not very popular with the PE teachers, and you can guess who was the butt of the jokes for the next little while.

Well, the chickens did come home to roost, eventually. It was a month later when we held our annual Christmas party and gag gift exchange. I could sense something was up, as there were many smiles and giggles aimed my way. When it was time to open my gift, I was so pleased because I had the "biggest" present of anyone there.

When I began to open it, I heard something inside. When it started clucking, it struck me as to what my present was. It had wings and a beak and was very much alive. I don't know the exact fate of that particular bird, but I recall our librarian asking if he could take it home with him.

The Berlin Marathon

Let me preface this by stating that the only things the following adventure shares with the actual Marathon Race in Germany are that they both did occur in Berlin, and they involved running for 3+ hours. It was not a race I trained for or even entered, and it wasn't until after I had completed it that I was even aware of having run in it. You may be a little confused by now, so let's back up to the start.

As part of my duties as deputy superintendent with the Prairie Rose School Division, I was responsible for staff supervision. Ralston School is a Kindergarten through nine-school with a unique make-up, having a large percentage of British students enrolled. The British Army uses the Suffield Training area to prepare British soldiers for wartime combat. The Ralston School was the only place out of 50 locations worldwide where the British students received a curriculum that was not British. These students receive instruction involving the Alberta curriculum.

To ensure continuity and the ability for these students to successfully integrate once they returned to the UK, I was "forced" to travel to Germany each year. Along with the Ralston School principal, we were required to attend a one-week conference where we were exposed to the major objectives of the British curriculum. Leaders of the schools where army children attended would gather to share educational strategies and techniques.

Each year, we would plan our flight to land in different German cities. If we had to work that far away from home, we decided to try to build a little pleasure in, along with ALL the business and work. Ok, you caught me in a little white lie. It wasn't "all work and no play." it was one of the greatest perks that I experienced in my entire work career.

Two weeks before we were to board our plane for Berlin, my travel partner was stricken with a "minor" heart attack. While he did fully recover, he could not accompany me, so I was on my own. I arrived in Berlin at 10:00 in the morning, so jet-lagged I could barely keep my eyes open. I took a cab to the hotel to unload my luggage. Knowing I had to get my internal body clock adjusted, I decided to do some sightseeing for the afternoon and evening since I would be leaving the following day.

I took a cab ride downtown to the Berlin Wall, the little bit of it left. It was about a 20-minute ride that covered some five kilometers. It was not what I would consider within walking distance. I visited the museum, which depicted items related to how desperate people had attempted to cross the wall to escape to West Berlin. Many were captured and returned to the East Side. Some disappeared forever.

When it was initially built, the wall went up overnight. If you happened to be visiting someone on the other side and spent the night, when you got up in the morning, you were unable to return home. The wall separated the East and West for 28 years.

After visiting the museum, I also spent some time in and around the Brandenburg Gate. For supper, I found a trendy German café where I had an authentic wiener schnitzel along with some quality alt ale. By then, I was exhausted, so I took another cab back to the hotel, where I pitted in for the night.

The next morning, I awoke refreshed, and since I wasn't leaving until after lunch, I decided to go for a short jog. Dressed in my shorts and tee-shirt, I left the hotel. I didn't bother to bring any money since I was not planning on being gone long. Those who have traveled to

Germany know they don't want you taking the room key with you. The key is usually on the end of a 5-kilogram doorstop to ensure you drop it at the desk before you leave. It can be picked up when you return.

I ran for about 15 minutes and came to a lush, green park filled with trees. I couldn't pass up the opportunity to feel the soft grass under my sneakers. I ran for about five minutes, and when I turned around, I observed several paths leading back out of the park. Being a decisive leader, I chose the one I thought I had taken and quickly discovered that I was in a strange part of town and nothing looked familiar.

I tried stopping a few people to ask for directions. The ones I talked to did not know much English. The other problem was that the hotel's name was about 38 letters long, and the only thing I remembered was the name started with a B. I didn't have money or a credit card to take a cab, and even if I had, I had no clue where we needed to go.

I felt my only option was to keep running until hopefully, I might see something familiar. Two hours later, I finally spotted something I recognized. It was the Brandenburg Gate. The one I had taken a 20-minute cab ride to the day before. At least I now knew the correct direction to go back, and an hour later, I drug my tired butt into my hotel.

We had picked this hotel to stay at because it was less than a block away from the train station. The destination of the conference I was attending was in Guttersloh. This was approximately a 4-hour train ride from Berlin.

I left the hotel, pulling my suitcase behind me. I was more than a little tired after my unscheduled morning marathon. Little did I realize that my trip was about to get a lot longer and more interesting than I could have ever imagined.

And You Thought Hitchhiking Was Dangerous

Just when you think, things can't get any worse, sometimes, they do. After getting lost in the morning and running all around Berlin, I just wanted to get on a train and get out of "Dodge." It was only a one-block walk to the train station from my hotel. I had wanted to leave around noon, but by now, it was already after 1:00 pm. After the crazy morning spent searching for my hotel, I was a little cranky. I just wanted to get on the train and try to catch some sleep.

When I arrived at the train station platform, there was not a ticket booth to be found. I knew the trains came and left on the hour and figured that with any luck, I could still be in Guttersloh well before supper. As I walked along, I spotted stairs leading down to another platform. I didn't realize until later that the tracks down there were for the subway. There were probably signs indicating where the tickets could be purchased, but since I didn't understand a lot of German, I must have missed them. Using typical man logic, I knew I would eventually find what I was looking for.

As I was walking, it occurred that this was not the spot where a ticket office should be located. The area was not very well lit, and there wasn't a lot of foot traffic. When I finally came to a small kiosk, I looked inside and spotted one man sitting behind a computer. When I told him that I needed to travel to Guttersloh, he looked at me quizzically and in broken English stated that this was a strange request.

He looked down at his computer, and after typing in a few things, I saw him smile. He said he couldn't get me to Guttersloh, but there was something to Bielefeld. From there, I could then take a taxi to my final destination. Before I could say or ask anything, he said, "You have to leave now, or you will miss your ride." When I asked him how much it would cost, he told me 15 Deutschmarks, which I quickly calculated to be $10. You probably think $10 to take a 4-hour train ride seems like too good of a deal, but I didn't have time to think.

He pointed to the platform's far end and told me to take the steps up. He scribbled out on a piece of paper a series of letters and numbers. It looked something like GSH42JL5934. At the top of the stairs, I would see the Deutsche Bank, and I was to wait there for the train. At least I thought I heard him say train. I went up the stairs, and there to my right was the bank.

I walked to the front of the bank and stopped to look around. There were no trains in sight. I did, however, spot a small car pulling up beside me. When I looked at the numbers and letters on the piece of paper in my hand, I immediately saw they were the same as the license plate on the car.

To say I was a little confused would be pretty accurate. A young guy jumped out from the driver's seat. In broken English, he asked if I was going to Bielefeld. When I shook my head yes, he opened the trunk. He moved a case of Pic a Pop bottles, grabbed my suitcase, and placed it inside. When he ran back to his side of the car and told me to hop in, I was still in shock and wondering what the h#$% was happening. I can't believe I am admitting this, but I got in the car, and we took off.

He had the radio blasting, and while I tried to ask him a few questions, it was apparent he was not comfortable with speaking English. It was at this point that I started to question my sanity. We drove for about 15 minutes before he pulled the car over to a stop where two guys were waiting. They didn't have any luggage, and when the vehicle stopped, the driver got out, and after saying a few things to them in German, they all entered the car.

So now, there I was, with three German strangers, traveling in a car, somewhere. By this time, many things were racing through my mind. I had visions of three drug dealers taking me out to some isolated area and disposing of my body in a shallow grave. There would be no witnesses of where I was or what I had been doing before my death. The one saving grace was that from how they talked, none of them seemed to know each other.

As we drove along the Autobahn, I had lots of time to think, which was not a good thing. After about an hour of driving, the car took an exit ramp that was NOT going to the place I wanted to go. I am sure the driver saw the panic on my face and pointed to one of the guys in the back and said, "Out." At first, I thought he was telling me to get out. I quickly discovered he wasn't talking to me. We had arrived at the destination of one of the backseat travelers. He thanked the driver and got out. We were soon back on the Autobahn to continue our journey. A half-hour later, we dropped off the other passenger, and it was just the two of us left for the last couple of hours.

I was pretty confused by all this and tried asking the driver what was going on. When he smiled and nodded and pulled the car over, I was unsure of what was happening next. He jumped out and motioned for me to drive. I was obviously not very good at charades if that was the message that he got from my hand gestures. I vigorously shook my head no that I didn't want to drive, and he got back in, and we took off again.

Four hours later, we had arrived at Bielefeld. Since he was getting ready to drop me off, I asked if he could drop me at a taxi stand because I still needed to get to Gutersloh. He smiled, and as it turned out, he was going through Gutersloh as well, so he just kept on driving.

I had the address of where I was staying, and he drove me right to the door. When I thanked him, I took out my wallet and tried to give him a tip for the door-to-door service. After all, I had only paid $10 for the trip I later found out should have cost $100. He shook his head no, but I took out 20 marks and laid it on the seat as I got out. I waved as he drove off. All I could think to myself was, "What the hell had just happened over the last four hours?"

I talked to several people afterward about my adventure. Most of them just shook their heads and had no idea what I was talking about. Finally, someone told me what had occurred.

It was a service where a person phones a company to tell them they are going to a specific destination and have room for passengers. All they charge is a little gas money. The odds of me wanting to go to a place four hours away and being in the right spot at the right time to make the connection were unbelievable. Looking back, it was not one of the most brilliant things I have ever done. I didn't even hitchhike when I was young and dumb. What was I thinking? You're right, I wasn't thinking, but isn't that how the best stories and memories are made?

Looking back, I missed the opportunity of a lifetime. If I had brought this idea back to North America and called it Uber, I could have become wealthy beyond my wildest dreams.

Excuse Me, But Have We Met Before

My first visit to the legendary city of Amsterdam came during the same trip, which began with me getting lost in Berlin, and accidentally hitchhiking to Gutersloh. I had managed to navigate halfway across Germany through a series of misadventures.

Once I had reached my conference destination, travel became much more relaxing. For the next six days, various hosts drove me to the schools we visited. All I had to do was sit back, relax, and enjoy the sights and sounds of the German countryside. I must admit that it was much less stressful riding with a driver I knew and who could speak English. I never once thought about being mugged and left to die in a ditch.

I had planned to return to Canada, flying out of the Schipol Airport in Amsterdam. Having never been to Amsterdam before, my hosts assured me they would make sure I got on an actual train which would safely transport me the 500 kilometers to my destination. I have to admit it was an enjoyable ride with occasional stops along the way. It was just after lunch when we pulled into the Centraal Station in downtown Amsterdam.

Having spent ten years living in Calgary, I assumed the only way to get to the airport was to take a taxi. I exited the train station and immediately spotted a long line of taxis. I had no problem finding one to take me to the airport. When I told the driver where I wanted to go, I thought I saw his eyes light up, and a smile cross his face. As we drove, I kept watching the meter clicking from $10 to $20 to $30 and wondering how much further we had to go. A $100 later, we arrived at my hotel near the Schipol Airport. That is about the same price I paid to take the train from Germany to Amsterdam.

I decided to have lunch at the hotel before spending the afternoon and evening sightseeing in Amsterdam. I debated whether I wanted to spend another $100 to get back downtown and another $100 to return. When I told the waiter my dilemma, he burst out laughing.

He informed me I could take the free bus shuttle right outside the hotel, and it was a 10-minute ride to the airport. I could jump on the train from the airport, and for $3, it would take me all the way downtown. This is the same train I left to get in a taxi. I was ok with saving $194 and was soon on my way to the most fascinating city I have ever visited. New Orleans is the one other city I would classify in that same category as very "interesting."

While waiting for the bus, I was standing alongside two other gentlemen. What happened while we were waiting highlighted the importance of learning different languages. Most of us in Canada and the United States are light years behind when it comes to being able to communicate in a different language. One of the men asked the other man a question. I wasn't sure what language it was, but the other guy shook his head no and said something back in a different language. The first guy also shook his head no and came out with another language. The third time was a charm as they had finally found a language, they both knew. It is not uncommon for the average citizen in Holland to know three or four different languages.

This time there was no problem finding the train, and soon, I was right back at the Centraal Station, in the heart of downtown Amsterdam. When you exit the station, the first thing you see is a parking area filled with thousands of bicycles, as far as the eye can see. Bikes are the vehicle of choice in much of Holland, and Amsterdam is no exception.

In New York or Paris, you have to worry about getting run over by a cab. In Amsterdam, the chances of you getting hit by a bike are much higher than by a taxi. It is like watching NASCAR with the hundreds of people walking along streets and bicycles weaving in and out, ringing the little bells on their handlebars to clear the path ahead. I quickly learned NOT to move to the right if I heard a bell behind. This was the signal that a bicycle was about to pass.

People of all ages and sizes ride their bikes. There are even couples with the girl sitting side-saddle on the carrier over the back wheel. I found it interesting that when the bikes are parked, they are not chained up. I asked someone how they could find their bike amongst the thousands parked there. You need to know that most of these bikes are old, and the standard equipment is two wheels, a seat, handlebars, and a bell.

They don't spend a lot of time looking for their bike. They can generally quickly find one that looks similar and ride away on that bicycle. Who knows, next time they are back, they might find their original bike again.

I had one other learning experience with the Amsterdam train system, but this came on a different trip when Irene was with me. We had rented a car and found a hotel outside of the city. The last thing I wanted to do was drive downtown. The city is built in circles, and there are canals everywhere. Parking is at such a premium that if you are ever lucky enough to find a spot, they do not come cheaply.

We set off in the morning with our plan to take the train downtown and spend the day doing all the touristy things. It was Irene's first trip and my third, so I figured I was pretty much a tour guide by now. As we were riding along, we were talking about going to see Anne Frank's House, the Van Gogh Museum, and of course, the Red-Light District.

I noticed out of the corner of my eye that there was a young fellow, probably in his mid-20s, who was riding by himself and looking at us. He smiled, and we ended up talking to him. He told us that he worked in Utrecht, a city adjacent to Amsterdam. He told us something that would later become very prophetic. His exact words were, "Amsterdam is a friendly city, so don't be surprised if you meet someone you know."

The train had several stops, and when we came to one of the stations, he got up to get off. When he saw we weren't moving, he told us that this is where we had to get off and catch another train that would take us downtown. We thanked him for his help and were off to see the sights.

We had a great day, and 10 hours later, after a lot of walking, we were dragging our butts. We got off the first train and were waiting for the next train to take us back to our hotel. As we were getting ready to board one of the approaching trains, we heard a voice behind us say, "You don't want to get on that train." When we turned around, it was the same guy we had spoken to that morning. He had returned from his day of work and was waiting for the same train.

I am not sure what the odds were of his saving us twice in one day, but he was absolutely correct. In Amsterdam, you can run into someone you know.

Work Sets You Free

No one should ever think life is easy and we should never be surprised when it does not seem fair. There are some places you visit, in the world, that are so beautiful, you hope to remember them forever. And on the other hand, there are those places so horrific that you can never forget them. Over the years, I have had the opportunity to witness examples of both of these. While I can NEVER unsee the devastation of evil that has sometimes occurred, it is essential to remember, so that civilization doesn't ever make the same mistake again.

Growing up, two of the most impactful movies I have ever seen are Schindler's List and Sofie's Choice. Both are set in Europe, during the regime of the Nazis. In the 1940s, Schindler acquired an enamelware factory in Kraków, Poland. Risking his own life, he helped protect his Jewish workers and saved hundreds of them from deportation and death in the Nazi concentration camps.

Sofie's Choice cannot be connected to a specific person, but was based on a story told by a refugee from Poland who had escaped Auschwitz, the largest extermination camp. Over a million people were put to death there over a brief period of two years. At the whim of a cruel guard, Sophie was forced to make a spontaneous decision as to which of her two children lived and which would be put to death. Atrocities such as this can only flourish when power has corrupted those in charge and when decisions about the value of human life are made based on ethnicity or background.

There were a number of these death camps located in Germany, and today, they serve as a reminder of all the abominations of human genocide. I have personally visited two of these camps and will attempt to describe my feelings and memories in a way that does justice to the importance of what they stand for.

The first camp I visited was Dachau, located outside of Munich. Before the era of the Nazis, these camps were called concentration camps. The more appropriate term utilized after the war was death camps. When you enter the compound, the first thing you observe is a large sign with the slogan "Arbeit Macht Frei." Loosely translated, this means "Work sets you free." For most of those incarcerated there, the truth was that you would only be free once you had been worked to death. While the camp was not built for the same purposes of extermination as others, such as Auschwitz, the conditions were so brutal that most people died long before they were liberated.

There are several original buildings still standing. The structures that housed the prisoners are stark halls with wooden bunks filling most of the area. They were built to hold 6000 people and were usually occupied by up to 30 000, with five people sharing one bunk bed.

Although there is a gas chamber built on the site, it was not used for extermination. Or so they say. Individuals that were determined to be unfit for forced labour were sent to Hartheim Castle, where they ended up in the gas chamber. Most of the people murdered at Dachau were executed either by a firing squad or hanging. There are rooms with large hooks on the wall where people were hung on display to remind the others of the importance of following the rules.

The day we visited Dachau was overcast with a drizzling rain. The only thing more depressing than the weather was the face of every visitor we passed. It was impossible to look at all the pictures and read the stories without tears coming to your eyes. It was not uncommon to hear loud sobbing and wailing as someone would reach their breaking point.

We ended up walking through a small room where a Catholic Mass was being celebrated in German. There were only a dozen people in the congregation, so we joined them. There were no pews or chairs, so we stood along with the others. Although we couldn't understand a word the priest said, we stayed for the entire service and even shared in Communion. I have never experienced a more powerful feeling from attending church than I did on that day. If Disneyland is the "Happiest Place on Earth," then Dachau must be the "Saddest Place on Earth."

After Dachau, I swore that while it had to be seen once, I never wanted another experience like that. However, during my visits to Amsterdam, I always felt compelled to visit the Anne Frank house. I have done the tour through the house three times now and will go again if I ever get back there. This house was where Anne and seven other family members hid out from the Germans in an upstairs apartment, no bigger than 450 square feet.

For 25 months, they could not make any noise or leave the building. When an anonymous informant revealed their presence to the authorities, Anne and her sister, Margot Frank, were sent to Auschwitz. In what only could be described as an act of God, they somehow escaped the gas chambers and were transferred to Bergen-Belsen. This concentration camp was located in northern Germany. In February 1945, the Frank sisters died of typhus at Bergen-Belsen, and their bodies were thrown into a mass grave. It was only two months later that the camp was liberated, and they would have been set free.

While this camp was not as notorious as Dachau or Auschwitz, there was still the ever-present feeling of evil and helplessness that permeated throughout. I can remember the silence more than anything. No one spoke above a whisper, and there were no birds, animals, or flowers around to break the eerie silence. It was very apparent that the present-day German citizens do not like to talk about what happened there.

It serves as a highly unpleasant reminder of what can happen when one segment of society chooses to ignore or refute what is happening around them. Whenever I hear Peter, Paul and Mary sing *Where have All the Flowers Gone*, I think to myself, "When Will We Ever Learn."

Zimmer Frei

While I have always tried to be as planned as possible, when it comes to travel arrangements, I would be the first to admit it is often the "surprises" that we remember the most. These surprises can occur because of a wrong turn, a cultural difference that we could not predict, or even just being in the wrong place at the right time.

When we traveled around Germany, we generally avoided hotels. We preferred staying in bed and breakfasts where you could experience the locals and their history. When you drive through any small town, you will see signs outside of houses that say, Zimmer Frei. It does not mean Mr. and Mrs. Zimmer live there. It is the German way of saying there is a room available for overnight accommodation.

The Germans are well known for their cleanliness and attention to detail. We were never disappointed with any of the B and B's where we stayed. Along with an immaculate room, we were treated to some fantastic breakfasts and always a little history and some local stories.

Another unanticipated bonus was that you never knew what kind of plumbing system you would encounter. There are probably more types of flush toilets and showers in Germany than anywhere else in the world. Often, we had to search around to find what to push and flush. And the variety of showers often resulted in moments of scalding water followed by an icy cold blast immediately after.

The only downside we quickly discovered with the Zimmers was that most of these rooms were not available on Sundays. The families often took off this one day a week for themselves. We were then forced to find alternative accommodations. There was absolutely nothing wrong with most of the hotels. It was just that you didn't get the personal experience of living with the locals.

On one of these Sundays, we ended up in a surprising and very memorable situation for all of us involved. When we checked into our hotel that afternoon, we asked the attendant if any Oktoberfest type activities going on. While his English was much better than our German, I am not sure he knew quite what we were looking for. He made hand gestures of drinking and eating and made a little map for us, showing how to get to this "party."

When we drove up to the hall, there were many cars in the parking lot, and several people were directing us where to park. As we walked into the large gathering room, we were greeted with smiles and a friendly "Gutentag" welcome. We chose a small table that was vacant and sat down. I went over to get us a couple of beer and was pleasantly surprised at how inexpensive the drinks were.

At the front of the hall, on stage, there was a single performer who could best be described as a one-man-band. He was wearing the traditional German Lederhosen, of leather shorts and suspenders. He played the accordion and had a set of cymbals between his knees. He was belting out polka music that had everyone tapping their toes.

The one thing we had discovered in our travels was that once you got off the Autobahn and visited the small towns, most of the people spoke very little English. The exception was that many of the younger generation took English as part of their school studies.

While we were sitting, drinking our beer, a group of teenagers was beside us. We noticed them looking at us and smiling as they heard us talking English. I think they felt this was an opportunity to practice their English skills. After some polite exchanges, they asked us a question we were NOT expecting. They pointed to a board at the side, divided in half with pictures and names on either side.

Their question was, which side of the family did we belong to? While no one ever told us to leave, it was a little uncomfortable, knowing we were crashing a family reunion. We ended up leaving a short time later to go back to the hotel for the evening.

For the rest of the trip, we never crashed any other private functions. However, we did expand our horizons in terms of new cultural experiences. The first of these occurred when we stayed in a small village that looked like a picture out of a storybook. While strolling around the town, we came to a small church surrounded by a graveyard.

The churchyards are often where local parishioners are buried. In walking around the church, we noticed a freshly dug grave with the dirt still piled up beside it. When we rounded a corner, we came upon an overhang, covering an ornate coffin, with the lid closed. I immediately looked at Irene and told her to get ready to take my picture as I would go over and open the top to see what or who was inside.

Not bloody likely. I have no idea whether there was a body inside, but the last thing I wanted was to desecrate a sacred burial site. We ran, not walked, away as fast as we could.

Another interesting event occurred when we decided to get a loaf of bread, some cold cuts and cheese, and a bottle of vino. We had found a beautiful little park and decided to "do what the locals do." That being, enjoying a picnic in the park. Others were doing the same, so we knew it must have been legal to drink in a public area.

We were sitting, enjoying the beautiful weather and the treats when three people moved in beside us. It appeared to be an elderly couple and their 40 something daughter. They spread out a blanket to sit on. They proceeded to take off their clothes to get a bit of a tan. It is a common practice for women to go topless, but I believe there should be an age restriction on this. I understand I have no right to make a judgment on this. However, I had to smile as I thought of the old saying that "spandex is a privilege, not a right."

One thing about traveling is you never know when you might meet some fascinating people. One night we stopped at a restaurant that had a unique patio arrangement. All the tables around the sides had a roof covering them. There were a few tables in the middle, where we were sitting, that had nothing but the sky above. When it started to rain, our table was the only one getting wet. A lovely couple beside us waved us over to join them. It didn't take them long to realize that their kindness resulted in an evening of far more work than they had anticipated. With neither of us speaking each other's language, we had to resort to charades and hand gestures to hold a polite conversation. As they say, no good deed goes unpunished.

Abs of Steel

Hypnosis is an altered state of mind or trance, marked by a level of awareness different from the ordinary state of consciousness. Hypnotized subjects are said to show an increased response to suggestions. Hypnosis usually begins with a hypnotic induction involving a series of preliminary instructions. Hypnotism as a form of entertainment for an audience is known as "stage hypnosis," a form of mentalism.

Do you believe hypnosis is for real? I certainly didn't. How could anyone "make" me do something against my will. Over the years, I had watched different hypnotists on television and was very entertained at how they could get their subjects to do the wildest things.

The first hypnotist I saw in person was Peter Reveen, aka "Reveen." Dad packed up the whole family for a night of entertainment at the old Paramount Theatre in Lethbridge. I was stoked and determined that I wanted to be hypnotized. I can remember closing my eyes and concentrating on his every word. When he instructed us to open our eyes….NOTHING. I wasn't in a trance, and my plans of instant fame, on the stage of the Paramount, came to a crashing end.

Reveen performed a family rated show, although he did throw in the occasional racy suggestion. He always stopped the performers before they removed any clothing of importance. I remember him putting the people into and out of a trance by merely snapping his fingers.

He would have people go back to their seats in the audience, and when he said the "magic" word, they would come screaming down the aisle. They were frantic and trying to warn everyone that aliens had landed and we were all going to be abducted. It all seemed so scripted that I couldn't believe it was not a setup. I was convinced that they were actors, paid to entertain the audience.

My thoughts about hypnosis changed one summer during our annual superintendent's conference in Waterton. There were about 150 people packed into the tiny community hall in Waterton. It could comfortably house 100, so it provided a very intimate, non-social distancing environment. Ed, a school superintendent from Northern Alberta, was the keynote entertainment for the evening. As a sideline, he practiced hypnosis and was highly sought after to perform at gatherings around the province. Since I knew him reasonably well, I was very skeptical about how skilled he might be. Heck, he was a regular guy, just like one of us.

He started the show in the usual way with an audience participation event to identify the potential entertainers for the evening. He instructed everyone to close their eyes and concentrate only on his voice. He spoke softly, continually suggesting that we were delving deeper and deeper into our consciousness. After several minutes of "suggestion," he told us that our right arm was going to suddenly become so light that it would feel like it was floating away. This was followed by another suggestion that our left arm would feel so heavy that we couldn't hold it up anymore. This whole time, Ed was looking around the audience and observing which "victims" he would be inviting on to the stage. When he told us to open our eyes, he stared directly at me. He smiled, and with his crooked finger, he was beckoning me up to the stage. When I looked at my hands, the one was down at my side, and the other reached up to the ceiling. It was too late to try to claim I wasn't hypnotized.

There ended up being a dozen of us up on the stage. We were not all "under" at the same time. I remember watching people doing some things I was glad I was not doing. However, there were also significant gaps when I was doing activities that the others were happy that they weren't doing. I can remember doing a "mean" Elvis impersonation, and I swear I sounded exactly like the real deal. Who would have known these old hips could still move like that.

I also recall trying to swim across the stage because the ship we were on was sinking. During one of the acts, I was informed that I could not say the number seven. It seemed every time it was my turn to call out a number, it was a seven. As hard as I tried, I couldn't make my mouth say the number. A couple of times, I tried to get close by saying six or eight, but then I was severely chastised by Ed for not telling the truth.

Because I was in such a deep trance, Ed decided to try something, for the finale, that he usually would not have done. He decided I would be the star guinea pig, who would end the evening with a bang. By this time, I was the only one left on stage, and Ed was explaining to the audience that he had only attempted this a couple of times before, but he was confident it would be successful.

I was instructed to stand beside him, with my arms at my side. He began suggesting that my body was becoming more and more rigid, and I was turning into a rod of steel. The more he talked, the tighter I could feel my arms pressing into my sides until finally, I was convinced that my body was frozen with paralysis. He placed two chairs my body length apart. With the help of a couple of volunteers, he put my head on one chair, and my feet were placed on the other chair. I was stretched straight out, only supported by my head and feet. If I. had any say in the matter, that would have been enough. For Ed, this was not good enough.

He called up a young girl from the audience, who I found out later was 12 years old. With Ed's help, she stepped onto my chest with one foot and then the other until I supported her entire weight. While this only lasted a few seconds, looking at it on tape, it seems like too long. I may have bent a little, but I didn't break.

When Ed snapped me out of the trance, I remember everyone cheering but had no idea why. He asked me to try to see if I could stretch across the chairs for him. If I got my head on the one chair, the other end sagged to the floor. Even with volunteer help, there was no way I could support just my body alone, let alone having anyone stand on me. For those of you who doubt this story, I do have a videotape that captured it for all time. Honestly, it hurts just watching the girl standing on my chest.

I remember Ed telling us, as we were waking up, that we would have the best sleep of our lives that night. We would wake up the next morning feeling more refreshed than ever before. To be truthful, I did not notice that I slept any better. However, there was one thing I could not believe. The show had started at 7:00 pm. I can remember waking up on stage and thinking that the show was just beginning. When I looked at my watch and saw that it was 9:00, I felt as if I had been the victim of alien abduction, and my memory had been erased. I guess that's two hours of my life, I'll never get back, but I did get my "15 minutes of fame on the stage".

Lowell's of the World, Unite

After many years of trying to bribe people into pre-buying my book, I have finally sold the very first copy of my soon-to-be-released autobiography, entitled "Lowell; the Man, the Myth, the Legend in his Own Mind." Thanks to our friends, Joe and Bev, for buying the first copy. I am now on my way to becoming a best-selling author. When Joe made his request, the first thing I thought was that he was just being kind and making a pity purchase. However, when he indicated he wanted and needed the book, I could feel my chest and head swell with pride.

As with most news, there is sometimes a but attached. I was quickly informed that the sale was dependent on two conditions being met. The first was that the book had to be as long as possible. A couple of thousand pages would be perfect. Also, he needed to receive his copy within the next couple of weeks. I thought that obviously, he must want the book very badly, so I put an immediate rush on it. Always looking for ways to improve, I had to ask the reasoning behind his two requests. He did not hesitate to tell me that he was running short of toilet paper, and at least he wouldn't feel guilty ripping the pages out of MY book in case of an emergency.

This is the perfect segway into the theme of this story which is "After toilet paper, what is the next most important thing we NEED during this time of quarantine?" And of course, we would all agree the one thing keeping us somewhat sane is having access to the internet. You can only watch so many reruns of the 1967 Stanley Cup finals between the Maple Leafs and Canadians. Not only was this Canada's 100th birthday, but it was also the last year the Leafs won the Stanley Cup. It looks like only 47 years before they could potentially challenge for another cup.

I bet at some point during this quarantine that you became so "stir crazy" that you googled your name just to see what came up. And if you didn't, you will NOW. If your name happens to be John Smith, chances are, you are still trying to narrow the search down. However, when your name is Lowell Leffler, there is a pretty good chance that whatever pops up, will in some way, be related to you.

I am not sure how the Google search engine works, but it seems pretty random about the things it brings up in its top ten. I don't remember specifically saving anything to the "Cloud." Still, it appears that anytime any document is saved or sent, there is a chance of it being tied to your profile in perpetuity. The three most important things I have ever published are the following:

The first is an article on how to correctly repair your divots on the green.

The second article was put out by the ATA in 2004, where I expressed ideas for improving student scores on Junior High Math Achievement Tests.

The last of my most memorable written accomplishments was a 1996 series of blogs written about me by a Grade 3 class of students at the Burdett School.

While all of these articles are potential Pulitzer Prize winners, I am still awaiting the Academy's call as to my nomination. The question I have is, "Who or what determines what will appear in a Google search, and can this ever be removed." I have not personally attempted to answer the above questions. I have, however, talked to people who were very upset because of the personal information that was posted and available by searching their names.

Specifics of a divorce settlement or pictures where they were captured in less than flattering situations are not something anyone wants the world to access. If you have read many of my early adventures, you will understand why I was so fortunate there were no cell phones or internet back then to capture those moments when MY brain went on pause.

You can't get away with stuff like that today, and you never know when something could come back to bite you in the butt. One of the most tragic situations I had to deal with, as an administrator, was when some parents discovered "compromising" pictures of their daughter's teacher online. It was a long and unpleasant process to work through, and while everyone is entitled to their own lives, what happens in Vegas doesn't always stay in Vegas.

If the internet and Cloud's permanency don't scare the heck out of you, you may be living in a fantasy world. It seems we are long past George Orwell's "1984" and Big Brother is alive and well, watching and recording.

This is not to say there are not some very positive uses for the internet. For example, thanks to the internet, I have decided to host the first annual "Lowell Leffler Namesake Reunion" once this pandemic is over. I will be inviting people from around the world, who share this name, to get together for a weekend of laughter, memories, and cheer. It will be held in Marion, Ohio, during the second week of August.

We will be meeting in Ohio because I could only find one other person with the same name, and that is where he grew up. He was a pilot and First Lieutenant who served with the 30th Bombardment Group (Heavy) in the U.S. Army Air Force. He was a WWII causality who ended up missing in action, so I didn't even have to ask if he wanted to meet me in Bow Island.

Maybe I should look into combining with another family, so it's not quite so lonely at the reunion. Any guesses as to how many Englebert Humperdinks there are in the world?

COVID-19 Pandemic

A Near Miss

One of the hardest things about getting older is admitting that you are no longer capable of the same things you did when you were younger. Some obvious examples include not hitting a golf ball as far as you used to or not being able to run at the same speed as you did 20 years ago. These are not life-threatening, but merely frustrating because they remind us that none of us can escape the certainty of aging.

I recently experienced a life-threatening incident and my stubbornness and resistance to admitting my decreased ability to perform almost ended with tragedy. I am writing this hoping that it might prevent something like this from ever happening to anyone else. If one friend or family member can glean anything from my experience, I will have accomplished something huge.

This incident happened during the recent Coronavirus scare. At the beginning of March, 2020, our insurance provider informed us that we had ten days to return to Canada from our Arizona home. In the past, we have always made this trip in two days. Generally, the first day involved driving 14 hours, followed by a second more leisurely day of nine hours. With all the hype of border closures and isolation, I felt that the sooner we returned, the better.

We left Arizona at around 5:15 am on a Sunday, and the trip was smooth and uneventful for the first nine hours. There was very little traffic in Phoenix or Las Vegas, so we made excellent time. We stopped for lunch at Mesquite and continued on our way, intending to reach Pocatello for the night. We were cruising along the I15 Interstate at around 135 km/hr, keeping up with traffic flow.

I had set the cruise control, and beside me, Irene was knitting. I can remember feeling lethargic after lunch. I thought if I ate a few chocolate Easter eggs, it would give me an energy boost. I was too damn stubborn to stop and take a break. I had done this drive many years now, and I was confident that the feeling of drowsiness would soon pass, just as it always did in the past.

The next thing I remembered was hearing a loud bang, and when my eyes snapped open, I was looking in the rear-view mirror, watching a large, plastic orange center divider rolling behind our vehicle. I am not sure how, but I pulled the steering wheel back into my lane and straightened the car out. I was in total shock and denial.

Irene looked up from her knitting when she heard the bang and had no idea what had just happened. All I could think to do was keep up with the traffic. The car was still driving fine, and I was so embarrassed and upset at what had just happened that I could not speak. I just kept going. Irene was speaking to me, but I had no clue about what she was saying. I can remember saying I can't believe we are still alive.

When I finally did pull over for gas, I was very apprehensive about looking at the front of the car to see the damage. I was relieved to see there was only some minor scuffing of the front quarter panel and no dents or breakage. No one can tell me that guardian angels don't exist.

It has taken a couple of days to process the entire incident and start to think logically about what had happened. I have been given a valuable lesson and a second chance. The ending could have been much different. I debated whether we should ever tell our kids or friends about this, as it is still extremely embarrassing for me to admit. However, if I can use this second chance to give anyone else a second chance, I will swallow all of my pride and machismo.

I promise to everyone who reads this that in the future if I am feeling tired, I will pull over and take a rest. I do not need to be chastised for this, as I am doing a pretty good job of beating myself up over it. I just do not want this or something worse to happen to anyone else.

IF YOU ARE FEELING TIRED WHILE DRIVING, PULL OVER!

Subtitles Can Be Educational

When we arrived back in Canada on March 15, 2020, we were informed at the Canada/US border that we would have to self isolate for the next 14 days. This meant not coming within six feet of anyone and staying inside the house. The only exception was that we were allowed to go out into the yard.

I couldn't believe how the time FLEW by. Yeah, right! Thank goodness for our Kobo e-readers and the fact that we could download books from the Shortgrass Bow Island Library. I almost feel guilty admitting that we only have to pay an annual membership fee of $15/year. With Irene and I each reading two books a week, it worked out to about 7 cents/book. We figured that if we took turns eating every other day, we should manage to balance our budget, even on a senior's fixed income. In case you haven't noticed, this is *sarcasm*. There is no better deal anywhere than this. Support your local library.

One of the things I could get used to is not going shopping, even for food. We would phone up one of the two stores in town and give them a list of groceries that we required. An hour or two later, the doorbell rang, and there was a box of groceries sitting on our step. When we asked about how to pay for these, they told us not to worry about it, as they knew where we lived. This is one of the perks of living in a small town and something that most big-box stores do not offer as a service.

The biggest downside of all this is not visiting our grandchildren. Even after ten days, we wonder once the quarantine ends, whether or not we will visit as the last thing we want to do is put any of them in danger.

All those parents concerned that their kids will be watching too much television, try this. Turn off the volume and put on the subtitles. Presto, your kids are now reading.

Smile everyone. We will get through this together.

World War III

My first blog ever ended up being a little more serious than pretty much all the rest of my stories. I did not want people to think that my making light of certain situations was an indication that I didn't take what was happening with the pandemic seriously. On the contrary, things were dire, and my way of coping with this was to laugh. I am not a professional psychologist, but I have heard that laughter is healthy for you. So, here we go.

One of my earliest memories was when I was about seven years old. My parents both worked, and I contracted a cold or flu and could not go to school. Since I didn't care much about school anyhow, I would jump at any chance I could to stay home and watch television. My Aunt lived several houses away and was responsible for taking care of us if we could not go to school. If we were not too ill, we could stay home alone, and she would come over periodically to check on us.

In terms of today's parenting standards, this would not be considered acceptable behaviour. Then again, seatbelts were an option in cars until 1964, and it wasn't until years later that people actually used them. Fifty years ago, it was not uncommon for doctors and commercials to encourage smoking, especially for pregnant women, because it would help relax them from the stresses of childbearing.

While television did exist in the sixties, it was only black and white. You won't believe this, but we had to get up off the couch, walk over to the television and manually adjust the dial to control the volume and change channels. It was not a big deal because we only had one station to choose from.

I can remember one particular day as vividly as if it were yesterday. I was watching a movie about aliens attacking the Earth. They were trying to destroy humanity so they could take over. It was called *War of the Worlds*. This movie terrified me and left a lasting impression. I can remember looking up to the heavens for weeks after and checking to make sure that an armada of spaceships was not on their way to destroy us all.

In school, we learned there had been two World Wars in the past. World War I started in Austria and lasted from 1914 to 1918. World War II began when Germany invaded Poland and lasted from 1939 to 1945. Twenty million lives were lost in WWI, while more than 70 million people died during WWII. It was hoped that after such a devastating war, the human race had learned a lesson, and something like that could never happen again. And to date, it hasn't.

So here we are in the year 2020, fighting an enemy so small we can't see it without the use of an electron microscope. You may or may not know this, but Corona comes from Latin and refers to a part of the body resembling or likened to a crown. I was so relieved to discover that this virus was not related to Corona Beer and could not be spread through its consumption.

This is not your typical World War. We are no longer trying to kill our neighbours, although I get a little nervous from the looks Irene gives me when it is apparent that I am aggravating her last nerve. We are trying to save our neighbours by killing something that could ultimately destroy us. Can anyone else see the similarities here between the Coronavirus and attacking alien forces from outer space?

This is the first time the entire world has united to fight against something other than themselves. Being the eternal optimist, perhaps something good can come out of this chaos and confusion.

The song, *It's the end of the world as we know it* by REM is the most searched song on the Internet during this pandemic. I heard the lead singer, John Michael Stipe, discussing the lyrics' meaning. He indicated that it was not a song about the world ending, but rather the world-changing. There is no question things have changed already, and the world will be very different after this virus runs its course. The question that cannot be answered right now is how it is going to be different.

The answer to this question lies in each of us. As of December 2020, there have only been 1.6 million deaths linked to the Coronavirus. This number may seem small compared to the casualties from the other World Wars. A big part of this is because we as humans are getting smarter. Viruses do not have a brain. Their goal is simply to reproduce. It reminds me of teenage boys, throughout history and yes, I was one.

Viruses don't intentionally kill their host. Perhaps humans who do have a brain will realize that the only way we can survive and get better is to help rather than hinder, and love rather than hate. I hope and pray the result will be a better world for our grandchildren and future generations in the end. We all knew, in the back of our minds, that what we were doing up until now was not sustainable.

The Tipping Point

Pooping is not a modern phenomenon and has been around since the beginning of time. It is a biological function that operates on the principle that what goes in must come out. The earliest recorded evidence of fossilized poop dates back to Cro-Magnon Man. Scientists once used this name to refer to what is now called Early Modern Humans or Anatomically Modern Humans—people who lived in our world at the end of the last ice age (circa 40,000–10,000 years ago).

We are all familiar with Anno Domini (AD) and Before Christ (BC) used to label or number years in the Julian and Gregorian calendars. With the recent events, in grocery stores where hoarding of toilet paper has been the highest trending event, I propose a new system of dating. I will call this Before Charmin (BC) and After Dumping (AD).

Joseph Gayetty is credited with being the inventor of modern, commercially known toilet paper in the United States. Gayetty's paper, first introduced in 1857, was still available as late as the 1920s. Gayetty's Medicated Paper was sold in packages of flat sheets, watermarked with the inventor's name. Talk about the ultimate legacy to leave your children. Their name emblazoned on toilet paper.

I was born in Yorkton, Saskatchewan. We moved to Grassy Lake, Alberta, when I was only two years old. Most of my relatives stayed and farmed in South Eastern Saskatchewan, near the Manitoba border. I am not saying this was the Ozarks of Canada; however, one of my early memories includes the "party line" telephone, where my aunts could secretly listen to each other's telephone calls.

It was a form of early Facebook where everyone knew what everyone else was doing. If you wanted to get the news out, all you had to do was dial one of the phones, and everyone could "secretly" listen in. If you wanted privacy, you just had to say the name of a specific Aunt and tell her you knew she was listening. You would hear the little click as she hung up her phone, embarrassed because she knew she had been caught red-handed.

I will also never forget the two things I remember most about going to the bathroom at a very young age in Saskatchewan. The first was the old wooden outhouse, located far enough to ensure that the smell was not observable in the house. Yet, it still had to be close enough that it could be reached in the event of an emergency.

These outhouses were precariously perched over a deep hole that over time would fill up, resulting in the necessity to move it to a new location. While I was never actually convicted of "outhouse tipping," it was a common occurrence at Halloween. We, I mean someone, would tip the outhouse over. If an unsuspecting victim was not vigilant while running around in the dark, they sometimes would find themselves submerged in a smelly sludge collected over the last several months.

Most outhouses had two holes, placed precisely 24 inches apart. Initially, I was confused about why there was a need for two openings. The last thing I wanted to do during such an intimate and personal hygiene function was to have someone beside me to visit with. When I was old enough to stand on my own, I discovered that the seat on the left was designated for the *standers*. These were the men who could aim well enough that most of what they were eliminating ended up inside the circumference of the hole.

The reason for the left side was because they could use their left hand to steady themselves against the side of the outhouse and hopefully improve their aim. The right seat was the designated *sitters'* side, and may God help you if you accidentally left any evidence of your visit on the side where the ladies sat.

The most important item located within the outhouse was one of two things; either the Eaton's or Sears catalogues. My relatives could never afford to buy toilet paper or most of the things you could shop for in the catalogues. However, the pages could easily be torn out of the book and used as an excellent resource for wiping.

There was a very distinct protocol for the usage of the pages. Appliances and household items pages were used first. Next was the clothing section and finally the toy section. The reason the toys were last was that it was so difficult to get kids to use the outhouse that there had to be some bribery involved. It was easier to distract their attention if they could look and dream of all the new-fangled toys they could fantasize about.

Speaking of fantasizing, I now come to the clothing section I mentioned earlier. This section usually fell somewhere between pages 113 and 131 of most catalogues. Not that I would know from personal experience. It was, of course, every young boys' naughty desire.

I am talking about the ladies' lingerie section. Here you could observe actual brassieres worn by women with a propensity for cleavage. For those who are too young to remember, you need to know that all the underwear depicted was worn over outer clothing. To this very day, there is nothing sexier than a well-endowed woman wearing a bra over the top of a turtle neck sweater.

Earlier, I had talked about another early memory besides the outhouse. This was, of course, the five-gallon bucket located inside the closet of the adults of the house. When the weather was too cold outside or in the middle of the night, we were allowed to use the "Tin Throne" inside. Modern toilet training methods involve getting the kids to know when not to use their diapers.

Back in the old days, we had to learn balance first. Generally, the bucket was too high for us to put our feet on the floor, so we had to learn to center our little bums just right so we didn't fall into the bucket. Many a toddler from that era still has nightmares about the time when they slipped and had to be pulled out.

Cabbage Patch Casualties

I need to advance a disclaimer here and warn you that what you are about to read has been written by an older person who may be suffering somewhat from a receding social filter. Somehow, the elderly are blessed with a "get out of jail free" card. When an older person does or says something not politically correct, young people often assume that it results from our diminished mental capacities or advancing senility. In reality, many of us just don't give a crap and believe we have earned the right to say or do what we feel.

Over the years, I have survived several life-altering events, whereby shortages of something has resulted in us not getting those things we need or desire. In the grand scheme of things, the toilet paper shortage during COVID-19 is relatively low on the list of "events that were historically significant." Allow me to highlight some other seemingly end of the world scenarios I have suffered through and lived to see another day.

The most critical and earliest shortage I can remember occurred in Alberta during "The Beer Strike of 1985". It involved all local breweries stopping production for the next seven months. It was pandemonium in the streets as there was nary a liquor store to be found where you could purchase beer of any kind. I can remember my friends and I cruising past various liquor outlets in hopes of spotting the truck bringing in a rare shipment of beer from outside the province.

As soon as one of these was spotted, we had a fan-out phone system where everyone was immediately contacted and would swarm the truck and store involved. I can remember marching proudly out of the store with a 24 pack in each hand and watching the grief-stricken faces of those not lucky enough to snag any of the scarce products.

Things got so desperate during the dark months of '85 that we formed teams of convoys where we would travel to neighbouring Saskatchewan. The beer in Saskatchewan was pretty pricey and still is today, but at least you could get some.

Unfortunately, this was quickly figured out by the border patrol. We thought all they cared about was stopping the rats from entering Alberta. It soon became very dangerous to smuggle in this illegal libation. I have friends who were caught and imprisoned without due process, and while their prison sentences will soon be up, they will tell you if they had to do it over again, it was still worth the risk. I may have exaggerated a little about imprisonment.

Having survived the beer crisis, we were next faced with the gas shortage of the mid-90s. The oil industry had taken a big hit, and it was not uncommon to see line-ups of several hours with weary customers desperate to fill up their vehicles. There were many confirmed cases of *budgers* who would cut in front of people to speed their way through the lineup. Often fistfights and verbal assaults would ensue. I am not sure of the death toll attributed to this famine, but it was one of those times when I was happy not to run into anyone who was packing a pistol.

The most vicious and shocking events of all time occurred during the infamous Cabbage Patch Doll shortage of 1983 and the Tickle Me Elmo shortage of 1996. You talk about bloodshed. The mob massacres in Chicago had nothing over frantic parents searching for scarce Christmas presents. Panicked shoppers, Irene and I included, would line up for hours at our local Walmart with the hopes of snagging one of these elusive dolls.

There was no Facebook to help out, so we relied on radio news-casts or friends who happened to be in the right place at the right time. If a shipment had arrived in the store, the line-ups began the night before. When the doors opened the next morning, it was "All is fair in love and war." Many a doll was ripped in half by two adults fighting for possession.

Parents were convinced that if their children did not get one of these dolls, they would end up in counseling for the rest of their lives. I am happy to say that we were fortunate enough to be in the minority, lucky enough to acquire these items. Our kids, as a result, grew up relatively normal. Luckily for our kids, they inherited their "normal" genetics from their mother.

There are many other examples from history where the human race has suffered from product shortage. Examples like prohibition during the years 1918 – 1920 may have been seen by some to be of significant impact. It did result in job creation, even if most of it was illegal. I have not included any examples from before my time because they would all be second-hand and maybe not so accurate. I am sure you all know by now that I do not listen to gossip. In my world, it is always the "The Facts and only the facts, Ma'am" when it comes to my reporting.

The Devil is in the Detail

Who would have ever predicted or even believed the current highest social trending event? That being the hoarding of toilet paper. By scouring hundreds of Internet articles, I am the first person to solve the mystery of why there is not enough toilet paper to go around. The easy answer is hoarding. However, I will show you there is much more to the "real" truth. It is a conspiracy that was secretly planned years earlier.

I have noticed over the last few years that toilet paper rolls do not seem to be lasting as long as they used to. My first instinct was to blame this on my aging bladder and loose bowels. I will be the first to admit that age directly correlates to visits to the bathroom. However, I have discovered a much more insidious reason that toilet paper does not seem to go as far as it used to.

Historically, toilet paper rolls have been sold in rolls averaging 1000 sheets of one-ply or 500 sheets of two-plies per roll. Since I do not like the mess associated with one-ply tissue crumbling under pressure, I will base my findings on the two-plies. The dimensions of each sheet on a roll historically were consistent at 4.5 inches x 4.5 inches square. It averages out to 187.5 feet in length per roll.

While continuing to charge the same price, the toilet paper manufacturers have insidiously reduced the size of each sheet by 0.5 inches in width. As a result, each roll has a significantly smaller surface area of toilet paper on it. In some cases, it is a reduction of

26% less surface area that can be used to swipe up or down. While the roll may look the same size as before, it is now considerably smaller.

Through some meticulous measurements using only the latest advanced equipment, I have determined that the number of sheets necessary to adequately finish my cleanup after each BM averages around ten sheets. Please realize that I respect TP's value and have found ways to reduce the amount used. Not everyone may be doing the same. I would be very interested to hear from some of you as to whether or not this is a typical usage.

To ensure we are using the same constants and variables cogent to scientific investigatory techniques, we must compare apples to apples. I am willing to bet big bucks that people these days are much more aware of how much paper they are using compared to what they did a couple of months ago.

I find the process of cleanup generally involves a 3-stage triage.

The first round of *wipage* generally requires four sheets and involves getting rid of the largest and most abundant detritus. After each swipe, the sheets are folded in half, and the process is repeated. This can only be done a maximum of seven times. It is a scientific fact that when you take any sheet of paper of any size, you can only fold it seven times. After seven folds, the paper becomes so thick it is like trying to rip a phonebook in half.

Many of you will want to try this for yourself, so stop reading for a few moments and go try to fold any piece of paper in half eight times. I told you it couldn't be done.

The second round of *wipage* only requires three sheets as you are now more concerned with containment of the area and doing that broad sweep to ensure the majority of cleanup has been adequately performed. Please don't forget to fold the paper in half again each time.

Stage 3 of *wipage* should easily be accomplished by the remaining three sheets. At this point, we are looking for those areas that may be somewhat hidden or hard to reach. As they say, "the Devil is in the detail."

If I extrapolate my calculations, it would be reasonable to assume one roll of toilet paper should last me through 50 visits to the commode. Using the data based on the shrinking roll sizes, I reasonably could expect to adequately perform the job only 36.7 times. No one would want to round this off because you don't need to be a rocket scientist to figure out the mess involved there.

If we further extend this data over the 365 million people in Canada and the US, who require TP daily, you can see what "really" led to the crisis of toilet paper hoarding.

As you have discovered, I have a knack for digging up hidden facts that are both useless and trivial. However, I wish to close off this article by highlighting something related to the TP shortage that may have consequences more far-reaching than we could have ever imagined.

How many of you knew that the empty cardboard toilet paper roll is the most trusted instrument known to modern science when it comes to determining what *size* you need. Regular-sized *condoms* have almost the same circumference as the toilet paper tube. *Condoms* are a shade smaller, but a rolled-up *condom* is as big around as the end of a toilet paper tube. I don't think I have to explain the dangers of improperly sized condoms and the ramifications that would only be detected nine months later.

Hitting the Wall

In a previous story, I alluded to the fact that, in the past, I have run two marathons. A marathon is 26.2188 miles or 42.195 kilometers. During my training, I never actually ran that distance all at one time. Therefore, I was never sure I would have what it took to complete the entire run.

A superintendent friend of mine was a marathon runner, and when he heard I was training, he gave me some advice. He called it his "secret weapon." He warned me that no matter how much I trained or thought I was ready, there would come a time during the race when I would *hit the wall*. It is not easy to describe what this phenomenon truly feels like. The best way I can articulate the "wall" is for you to imagine yourself trying to run through quicksand while wearing lead shoes.

I ran my first marathon the year I turned 40. It was May 2, 1993, and I had flown into Vancouver the day before the race. It was May, and the sun was shining, and the weather was perfect, around 20 degrees Celsius. I don't remember the exact route, but I remember that we ran the first part of the race through Stanley Park. The atmosphere and scenery of the park were stunning. Along the route, people were running on stationary treadmills, bands were playing, and thousands of spectators cheered us on.

It doesn't take long to get into your rhythm, and soon you are running in a group of people who all have about the same pace. It was such an overwhelming experience that it almost seemed like I was on auto-pilot. I felt stronger and faster than at any other time in my entire life.

It was about the 13-mile mark, halfway, that we were breezing along, and I was chatting with a couple running beside me. I will never forget when the young lady turned to her husband and said, "We are making excellent time and should finish in less than three hours." This is when it hit me like a sledgehammer between the eyes. I was in deep trouble.

The most important thing about running a marathon is to pace yourself. During training, the longest run I did was 20 miles. My overall pace for that distance was 8.5 minutes per mile. When I heard the girl talk about three hours to completion, my mental calculations clarified that I was SCREWED. She was talking about running 7-minute miles.

Suddenly, I felt the earth tilt, and it seemed as if I was now running uphill. It was not a physical thing but completely mental. I had been so busy NOT thinking about running that I had gone out way too quickly. This, however, was NOT when I hit the wall.

I immediately slowed my pace down. Once again, I got into a rhythm, which lasted until about the 22-mile mark. My mind started playing tricks on me. I could clearly hear my brain screaming, "You have never run this far before" and "You have to stop NOW." When I looked up, all I could see was a long bridge ahead of me and an incline that seemed to go on forever.

That is when it hit me. I was going to "DIE" if I continued running. It is scary how powerful your mind is. I felt like I was only 100 feet away from scaling the top of Mount Everest, and I was going to have to stop and admit failure. Suddenly I remembered what my friend Mel had told me to do when I reached this stage.

I pulled over to the side of the road and bent over to my sock. Inside I had tucked a baggie with four secret weapons. These weapons go by the scientific name of Aspirin. I was to take a couple of these, but only if I was seriously contemplating quitting.

I ended up having to swallow the Aspirin dry since I was nowhere near a water station. I waited for the bolt of lightning that would hit me and pump new life into my aching muscles. When nothing happened, I decided that it might take a minute, so I began to jog slowly. I waited and waited, and my body felt the same as it did before I took the Aspirin. What I didn't notice was that I was so focused on my body, I forgot about my brain, and before I knew it, I was back running at a somewhat slower speed, but I was running.

Aspirin is not a "Magic Elixer," but what it did was settle my mind down, so it was no longer trying to sabotage me. I finished the race in 3 hours, 32 minutes, and 36 seconds. My pace was 8:11 min/mile. It was much better than I had ever dreamed possible. I didn't find out until after the race that I would have qualified for the Boston Marathon if I had run in under 3 hours and 30 min. So close. The Boston Marathon would have been my dream come true.

My second marathon was on May 6, 2001. I ran it along with my best friend, Hal. Growing up in a small town, we had shared many a beer and got into a lot of trouble together. To show you how close we were, he was my best man at our wedding, and I was his at his wedding., So it made sense to share this experience as well. My time was 3:36:15. Just a little slower than my previous race. I finished 626/3409 people who ran.

The point I am trying to make here is that we are all currently running a marathon together. I am, of course, referring to getting through this COVID-19 pandemic together. None of us were adequately trained for what we are currently trying to complete. At some point, we will hit the wall, whether it be some significant news event or just the mental state we find ourselves in.

I encourage everyone to think about a secret weapon you can pull out when it seems like the light at the end of the tunnel is a rapidly approaching locomotive. Maybe that secret weapon can be face timing with your loved ones, running on your treadmill, reading a book, knitting, or even just having a good laugh.

Consciously decide what you can use to help you keep on running and have it in your sock so you can use it when you see the "wall" coming. We WILL get through this.

I also learned a couple of other things during my race. The first being that if you want to peel and eat a banana, do it before you take a handful of Vaseline to rub on your inner thighs to prevent chafing. Also, when you are desperate, pride is often left behind. At one point, I had to make a quick trip into the bushes to relieve my bladder. When I looked around, a couple of women were squatting, and one man was standing beside me, doing the same thing as me. When you HAVE to go, and there is no bathroom around, your options become very limited.

Speaking of laughter, I saw the best tee-shirt in that marathon. I came up behind a runner, and on the back of their shirt, I read, "Please God let there be someone behind me to read this." No one wants to be last, but last is still better than not running the race.

I Used to Cough to Hide a Fart

After returning to Canada from Arizona, because of the pandemic, we were instructed at the border that we had to quarantine. I distinctly remember when finally, our 14-day self-isolating quarantine was completed. I am sure many of you would agree there could be some challenges during this 24/7 "quality time" that we get to spend together with only our loved ones.

I now have a better understanding of why the countries with the lowest impaired driver convictions are those where the penalty is a "life sentence," and your spouse is incarcerated with you. I also understand why some groups have called for a more humane punishment, such as the death penalty. I'm just kidding, Irene. It was not that bad. Honest. Ouch!

We so looked forward to our release knowing we had displayed good behaviour throughout the ordeal. It was ultimately proven that we were NOT guilty of the illegal transportation of deadly substances, also known as COVID-19 critters. We were not sure ourselves, so we held no grudges. I do not think we did anything to "flatten the curve." Au contraire, it has been far too easy to sneak into the cupboard to help fill the time, and as a result, many of my curves have grown much more pronounced.

I began to feel like the baby bird who had climbed to the side of the nest to peer out over the edge in terror. He had seen the others take the plunge, but he is not completely sure that he is ready. Would his little, untested wings or even a face mask and gloves stop him from becoming a road pizza? Eventually, I began to understand the motivation for the baby bird to finally take the plunge. In thinking like a bird, this self-isolation had made me realize that if I had to eat one more damn worm, I would be looking for a cliff to jump off.

To recap, let us look back at the time served. Our typical day began with sleeping in as late as we wanted. For me, it was 4:00 a.m. when I awoke. Irene would start to stir around 8:00 a.m. We would spend some time on Facebook and reading our email messages. This was followed by some physical exercise which included an hour on the treadmill. After working up an appetite, we ate our breakfast of two hard-boiled eggs and a small bowl of grapes.

Once our body's energy needs had been replenished, we settled in on our recliner/lounger for some reading on our Kobo's. Before you knew it, it was time to chop up our veggies for the daily lunch salad. By now, one of us had already been up for seven or eight hours, so it was time for a short nap of a couple of hours.

After waking, it was time for "happy hour." This involved a snack of some sort along with a libation of our choice. To avoid those extra calories from settling directly on our hips, another one hour on the elliptical was in order.

The day had flown by, and it was time for supper. We discovered a novel way to add a little variety to this meal. One of us would take a turn going to the freezer and moving the contents around. The other would get to play freezer roulette where they were blindfolded and whatever they grabbed onto became the meal du jour.

Once supper was consumed and the dishes were finished, it was time to watch a little telly. It wasn't long before, Arizona Midnight which is 8:00 pm, was approaching, and it was bedtime.

Can you believe in having to repeat the above process over and over again for 14 straight days? Wait a minute, that's precisely what we do every day of our retirement.

Being acutely aware of the telltale symptoms of the Coronavirus, we maintained a vigilant log of any health issues we experienced during our time of isolation. Fortunately, we never experienced a sore throat, a cough, or a fever.

We did become acutely aware of some other symptoms which have become noticeably more intense over the last several years. Upon waking, we have found it almost impossible to physically lift our bodies out of bed. It seemed like every joint and muscle in our bodies ached. Once we limped around for a bit, they eventually did loosen up a little.

Throughout the day, and especially after four cups of coffee in the morning and numerous glasses of water, we ended up having to go to the bathroom many, many times. We also found that sometimes our patience wore thin throughout the day, and there were times when we thought it best to maintain our social distancing until all thoughts of murder had passed.

When it was finally time to go to bed, we found our sleep was often interrupted by getting up to pee every couple of hours. The worst occurred when I was suddenly awakened by Irene elbowing me in the head and yelling that I better stop snoring if I knew what was good for me.

I did quite a bit of research into these symptoms, and in my non-professional judgment, this disorder is NOT contagious. That is the good news. The bad news is that the only known cure is death. However, take heart. Some people have been known to live to over 100 while exhibiting these symptoms for years.

The time finally came when we were free to venture out into the unknown world we had not been a part of for two whole weeks. We couldn't wait to jump in our car and watch no one walking down the sidewalks. We observed all the closed businesses we were not allowed to enter. And, of course, it was going to be exciting to finally get up to two meters away from another human being. For our American friends, that is 2.187 yards, so don't forget to bring along your measuring tape.

How has life changed because of COVID-19? The most significant difference is that before, in public, I would cough to hide a fart. Now, I fart to hide a cough.

Which Food Group Do Tide Pods Belong To

Who would have thought when we changed our clocks on March 8, 2020, that we would have moved from Mountain Standard Zone time to Twilight Zone time? On February 2, Groundhog Day came and went. Around March 8, it came and went, and on March 9, it came and went, and on and on. Does anyone else feel like Bill Murray, who was stuck reliving the same day over and over again for 33 years in the epic 1993 *Groundhog Day* movie?

I doubt that a month ago, anyone in my circle of family or friends would have predicted what lay ahead of us in the coming days. In the initial stages, before the declaration of a pandemic, we heard medical experts telling us to wash our hands and practice social distancing. Of course, there were always those who ignored the warnings until it became necessary to implement hefty fines and even jail time for those not adhering to the law.

I love a good conspiracy theory as much as the next guy, so, in the beginning, I must admit I had my doubts as to the actual severity of the situation and the possibility that this was all being overblown. Once the seriousness of it became apparent, I fully supported the fact we had to do whatever was necessary to keep people inside. It appears people have finally clued in and are staying home.

So, this begs the question. When will the curve be flat enough? Up to this point, no one was willing to suggest even a tentative date when we might start the slow integration back to everyday life outside the home. I heard people suggest that self-isolation may not end until the disease has been eradicated or we had a vaccine available.

In the first instance, this may NEVER happen, and as for the second, timelines of a minimum of 18 months have been suggested. If that means we have 18 more months of the past month ahead of us, I am worried that the mortality rate of husbands may start a new curve of their own.

I have no idea whether it will be politicians or medical personnel or some mainframe computer in the cloud, with a specific algorithm that will decide when we are allowed to de-isolate. The biggest fear I have is that these decisions will be based on the "lowest common denominator." Let me explain.

We have all experienced those teachers who operated on the principle that if something untoward happened in the classroom, the answer was to punish the "whole" class. If I remember correctly, those teachers were never considered by anyone to be their favourite teachers or even "good" teachers. Even as kids, we knew they were making the easy decision, the one that required the least amount of work or effort to solve.

Everyone knows treating people equally is not the fair or best way to do things. Unfortunately, in society today, thanks to some lawyers, it has become necessary for companies to issue warnings. Take-out coffee cups warn the customer that the liquid coffee just purchased is hot and should not be applied directly to the skin, or a burn could result. Also, we must make sure people understand that cleaning products should not be consumed because they could be detrimental to your health. REALLY?

I am starting to become very worried that my freedom will be compromised because someone, who thinks it is okay to eat Tide Pods, has to be protected from themselves.

I understand it is somewhat of a "slippery slope" when we decide whether or not it is going to be ok to do certain things in public. I have powerful feelings about my favourite sport that goes by the four-letter name of GOLF. Recently it was determined that golf is not an essential service, and just like attending a 500-person rave, it is far too dangerous to risk allowing people to participate.

My chances of contracting COVID-19 are not the same, driving myself down the middle of the fairway as they are from parking in a packed lot at Costco and waiting in line with a hundred other people to get into the doors to shop. Oh wait, it is not illegal to do the shopping. I am not suggesting golf is as essential as food. That's crazy. However, I am advocating that we need to start looking at what things we can do to meet the requirements of social distancing and allow people to get on with their lives.

In Norway and parts of the US, they practice safe social distancing, and their golf courses are open. They have the holes covered, so the flagpole does not have to be removed, and if your ball hits the cover, the putt is considered in the cup. They have also taken out the rakes from the bunkers and allowed only one person, unless you have the same address, to ride in a cart at one time.

Some of our local courses were looking at these very same restrictions to ensure no transfer of the virus is possible. The powers that be have decided someone might abuse these privileges and do something stupid to endanger themselves or others. Here we go again with the lowest common denominator, making the easy decision and treating everyone equally.

Please don't assume the worst of the worst and punish the whole class just because some idiot wants to eat a Tide Pod.

The Day I Dyed

Having never experienced quarantine before, it was inevitable some situations would arise that we didn't see coming. Irene has been my hairdresser for 20 plus years now. Not being able to access the services of a professional stylist during the pandemic has been of no consequence to my external appearance. Unfortunately, there was one other person in the house who was not quite as fortunate. I didn't know it, but if women do not get their hair coloured every six weeks, this strange grey colour starts appearing at the roots.

By the time the grey starts to become evident to the casual observer, it is incredible the desperate measures women will subject themselves to. When Irene asked me if I wanted to try something we had never done before, at first, I became very excited. However, when she explained that she needed me to colour her hair, panic quickly struck me.

We all know when our kids or grandkids became bored, one trick that always pleased them was bringing out the crayons or paints and letting them colour. Despite their initial resistance to the idea, the result was often a masterpiece that ended up being proudly displayed on the fridge for all to see.

Once the initial shock of Irene's request wore off, I have to admit my interest was immediately piqued. During the lockdown, all hairdressers were forced to close their businesses. Being in a small town and living close to Amy, Irene arranged a plan. The bottles of necessary colour were measured out and put in bottles that we could pick up from the step outside her home. Along with the dye were several pages of explicit instructions that were necessary to follow if I was to avoid having this procedure turned into a nightmare.

I am well aware of how women, and Irene, in particular, are very fussy about their appearance and especially their hair. The first thing I demanded was that we sign a contract that would free me from any liens or encumbrances related to a botched hairdo. It was not so much a prenup as a pre-tint. I had no illusions that this formal agreement would save me from the tempest that would strike if I somehow caused her hair to fall out. Knowing I had the law on my side, I donned my plastic gloves and started mixing colours.

The first thing I had to do was divide Irene's head into quadrants. Metaphorically only, of course. The task involved painting one quadrant at a time. I was to paint ONLY the roots, nothing else. Women seem to like different shades in their hair, as long as one of them isn't grey. Using a long-handled comb, I lifted a section of hair, exposing the roots, and began to attempt my best Leonardo da Vinci impression.

Like magic, the grey in the roots took on a dark luster, and it was time to do the next section. As soon as I released the hair from the comb, it all fell into the dye I had so liberally applied. So much for having highlights down the shaft of the follicles. I was supposed to continue the process, moving along one minuscule part at a time. As soon as I lifted some strands of hair, others moved in to take their place, covering the roots. It wasn't long before I had no clue where I started or where I had left to go.

The absolute worst part of this whole process was the area close to the forehead, sides, and ears. How was I supposed to know this stuff stained the skin a beautiful shade of black? There was no convincing Irene that this looked like a great suntan. A Rorschach inkblot test would be closer to the look I had achieved. I thought leopard prints were chic.

Like any good artist, I just kept painting until I ran out of paint. It was the longest 40 minutes of my life. I sweated less during the entire running of either of my marathons. After waiting 40 minutes to be absorbed into the hair, I sadly discovered we were only half done.

The next step involved colouring the hair, from the roots to the end of the strand, with a slightly lighter shade. This would only happen if there were any part of the hair strand that I hadn't already saturated with the previous dye. With most of the hair already plastered to the scalp, I wasn't sure if there would be any uncoloured hair left to coat.

Once again, I kept squeezing the paint out and massaging it into any hairs that looked lonely. When you hear the saying, only the hairdresser knows for sure; this hairdresser was clueless. After the final wash and rinse in the sink, it was time to feast our eyes on the finished product. Looking through sample areas of all four quadrants, I must admit most of the grey was gone. I won't say there were as many highlights of varying colour as she might have received from Amy, but desperate times require desperate measures.

I guess you can say that the circle is complete. Irene can also now tell people that she sleeps with her hairdresser.

Retirement

Buy High, Sell Low

When we retired in 2010, Irene and I never imagined that, with a bit of planning, there was a way to avoid the harsh realities of winter, cold, and snow for the rest of our lives. I have always been a sun worshipper. It was a constant struggle to survive a long winter, either bundled up, enjoying the crisp -40(either Fahrenheit or Celisus) weather, or languishing in the balmy, 22 Celsius comfort of the inside of your home.

When we discovered that my sister Wendy and her husband Rick were planning a trip to Arizona, with the possibility of looking to buy a property there, I joked that if they found anything, Irene and I would put in half. We could alternate taking turns visiting throughout the winter.

As a married couple, we had purchased a couple of properties over the years, but we were not real estate gurus. We always managed to buy when the prices were high and sell when the bottom had dropped out of the market. From all the reading I have done, this might be the reverse of what most investors aspire to accomplish. Sometimes it seemed we were the sole reason that housing values crashed because it always happened right after we purchased a property.

Doug, my friend, and boss used a different strategy for realty decisions. He preferred to buy when the prices were low and watch as the values steadily rose. Was that legal? Our friends, Paul and

Jane, were the first to buy a house in the land of eternal sunshine in Arizona, and it was not long after that Doug and Roberta purchased a home there as well. For a couple of years, Doug would describe his house on a golf course and tell me I should buy one. Of course, I ignored his advice, but sometimes there is a thing called dumb luck.

When my sister and brother-in-law returned from their vacation down south, they informed us that we could be the proud owners of half a home in Arizona for a little under $30 000. Of course, we wondered if there was running water, indoor toilets and electricity, included with the shack for that price. We had just bought a new car which cost $10 000 more than the price they quoted for half a house. When they told us that the place was only six years old, on a golf course with a double attached garage, we quickly checked the calendar to see if it was April 1 already.

They assured us that everything was legit and almost too good to believe. We decided to pull the trigger. Remember, this was going to be the first time in our lives that we would go against the grain and buy something when the price was low. We decided to break the mold and take the chance.

You have to remember that 2010 when we purchased the home, was during the time of the perfect storm. It was just after Fannie Mae and Freddie Mac's heyday, which were government-sponsored enterprises that participated in driving the mortgage crisis. Before the "housing crash" in the US, which began in 2008, houses were being sold with "nothing down" and made available to anyone with a pulse, regardless of income or ability to make monthly payments. When "the chickens came home to roost," houses in 2004 that had sold for $160 000 were abandoned, as the buyers had not invested any money initially and still owed most of their mortgage. It was cheaper to walk away from the house.

Not only were we able to pick up a home for $100 000 less than what it was initially valued at, but the Canadian dollar was also actually 3 cents higher than its US counterpart. A little different than currently, where the US dollar is 25 cents higher than the loonie. For the paltry sum of $30 000, we became the proud owners of half a home in Arizona.

We were involved with a short sale. This has nothing to do with time, as we made our offer in February 2010 and were not approved until July of the same year. A short sale means that the bank owns the house and is willing to accept a purchase offer less than what was owed by the original owner. In other words, the bank is cutting its losses and giving the house away at a fire sale price.

Although many abandoned houses were trashed by the previous owners, we were fortunate in that regard. With a paint job on the inside and the installation of lights and fans, the house was ready to live in. We spent the first year taking turns and sometimes living together with the Thurstons.

It was not that we didn't get along. We quickly realized that we both wanted to spend our winters in Arizona. If we were going to have visitors, we needed to have our separate places. Since we had not been together long, it was easy to divide the assets. The Thurstons bought a home across the fairway from us. We were still close enough to talk to each other from the backyards, yet we now each had our own homes.

On a different note, our home's current value, as of December 2020, is $175 000 and going up each month. Not a bad return on our investment. What did we do wrong to actually make a profit?

Always a Bridesmaid

I wrote the following blog at the end of March while we were in the throws of quarantine, and golf was not allowed.

The next hole-in-one that I score will bring my grand total up to .... ONE. Over the years, I have often told my colleagues, friends, and relatives if I have to GO, I want it to be on a golf course somewhere, immediately after scoring my first hole-in-one.

After thinking carefully about this death wish, I believe I may inadvertently be the reason for my not having ever scored an ACE. Let me explain to you the tremendous power of the human brain. Of course, most of you know that I am not speaking from personal experience. Over the years, based on many of the things I have done, very little thinking went into many of the decisions I made.

I will never forget a speech I attended by a speaker who came out of Saskatchewan. His name was Gary Gregor, and part of his claim to fame was working with the Saskatchewan Roughriders in the areas of motivation and psychology. Just to clarify, he had nothing to do with teaching them math and counting. All my Rider friends will understand what I am referring to.

Gary talked about the power of the human mind and how it will either help or sabotage us to ensure our self-imposed expectations are realized. He would suggest that if deep down inside, you believed you were a 60% student in school, during the test, your mind would "make" you pick incorrect answers to ensure that you did not score too much above the 60% mark.

The more he talked about this, the more I thought about my golf game. Every time I am having the game of my life and shooting the lights out, suddenly, my mind thinks, you are not that good a golfer to shoot that low score. The next thing you know, I have triple-bogeyed the next three holes. On the flip side, when I start with a horrible first three or four holes, all of a sudden, my mind says, "You are NOT that bad a golfer," and then I start hitting long and straight and even making a few putts. These observations about the power of the brain make a lot of sense. It would help explain why it is so difficult to improve your golf game.

The other phenomenon Gary talked about was that the brain cannot comprehend negative thoughts. If you think to yourself that you do NOT want to hit the ball out of bounds to the right, guess what usually happens? It never fails. You hit the ball straight right, out of bounds. Rather than say, I don't want to hit the ball in the sand, tell yourself you want to hit the ball onto the green.

It was shortly after listening to him that I had the only sub-par round of my life. I had to keep my mind off of thinking about the score. I concentrated on one shot at a time and tried to think only positive thoughts. It came down to the last hole, and I had a putt of about 12 feet left. If I made the putt, I finished my round at one-under-par. If I missed the putt, I ended up with par or worse, if I 3 or 4-putted. Believe it or not, I made the putt. I have never been able to replicate this feat, but it was as if I was on autopilot and the thought of missing the putt never even entered my mind.

As I stated at the beginning of this story, my goal has been to live long enough to score a hole in one. I am convinced that the reason I never get close to the pin on a par 3 is that my mind does not want me to die. I have decided to change my goal to be that I want to die celebrating my 15th ace.

The world record for holes-in-one by one person is 51, and there are even some people who have recorded two aces in the same round. I have two friends with multiple aces. Paul has 16, and Bruce has eight. You would think that if they were true friends, they would have had the decency to lend me a couple. Some people are so greedy. The closest I have come to a hole-in-one is to personally witness three other people scoring an ace. All of those all happened in the same year.

One of these cherished moments occurred during league play while I was golfing against Ross. I am not saying he is a sandbagger, but that day, as he was walking along, there was a steady stream of sand trailing behind him. I had to give him a stroke a hole because of his "high" handicap. The ironic part was that he was still beating me without the strokes, and after four holes, I was down 4 points.

The 5th hole of the Bow Island course is a par three, and I knew I could beat him overall if I could win the next five holes. He had kept the honours, the whole round, so when he shot first, it was a swift arrow through my heart. His ball went up and straight towards the pin. It hit and rolled and disappeared. Talk about adding insult to injury. Although, I have to admit it was a pretty shot to watch.

The next hole-in-one occurred while I worked the Founders Cup in Phoenix, Arizona. This tournament features all the best lady golfers in the world. I am not sure of the other two golfers, but I will never forget Guiliana Molinari from Italy. We got to the par-three, 17th hole, just as it was getting dark. Since the group ahead was still on the green, we had a little time to kill. This hole happened to be the "Car Hole," where a brand-new Buick was on display for anyone lucky enough to score the ace. The three golfers were goofing around and taking turns getting their picture taken with their "new car."

When Giuliana stepped up and hit her shot, there was no question from the first contact that this was a great shot. When the ball bounced twice and dropped into the hole, there was a lot of screaming and cheering from the crowd, the players, and the volunteers.

There were tears and hugs all around. What makes this so special is that women golfers do not earn anywhere near what their male counterparts make, so winning a car is a huge deal and not just another trophy to add to their collection.

The last hole-in-one that I witnessed was the most exciting of all. My friend, Harold and I were golfing with our wives on the Oasis Golf course, where we live all winter. We came to the 15th hole, a par three of about 175 yards. I had the honours; one of the few times I beat Harold on a hole. I swung first and struck a beautiful shot directly towards the pin. The green is elevated and slopes away, so once the ball goes over the crest, it disappears.

I was confident that the ball should be somewhere on the green. Harold addressed his ball and striped another beauty straight towards the pin. It looked to us like the worst-case scenario was that the two of us would be putting for birdies. As we pulled up alongside the green, all we could see was one ball about 10 feet away from the pin.

I tend to be the eternal pessimist. If there are two balls and one is directly behind a tree, it always seems that there is a 90% chance that the bad shot is mine. When I walked over to the ball on the green, I couldn't believe it. It was my ball, and I had a great chance at a birdie. Harold and I walked all around behind the green looking for his ball. It was nowhere to be found.

Immediately I began calculating, in my head, that with my birdie and Harold having to take two extra strokes for a lost ball, I was going to gain several strokes on this one hole alone. As I was busy counting "my chickens," I walked over to the pin to pull out the flag. The flagpole felt stuck, and when I looked down, I saw a ball jammed in the hole.

Harold was busy still looking for his ball. When I yelled that I found his ball, he was a little suspicious. I still think, to this day, he believes there is a chance I might have pulled the biggest prank ever by faking that hole-in-one. Just so I am completely transparent about this, only me and the Golf Gods know the truth.

The dumbest tradition ever invented is that the golfer scoring the Ace has to buy drinks for everyone else. In what universe does it make sense to punish someone for doing something well? It was probably started by a sore "loser," who was a lousy golfer and had no hope of ever accomplishing such a feat. Anyhow, after Harold scored his one, I was more than happy to eat and drink all night at his expense. I guess I am one of those "LOSERS."

It Could Only Happen to Me

The previous article about the holes-in-one was written two weeks before this one. One of the worst parts about the first lockdown in March and April was that all golf courses were closed due to health concerns. Finally, in May, it was deemed that golf courses could open as long as they implemented mandatory safety measures to prevent the spread of infection. Rakes were removed from sand traps, and only people from the same household could share a power cart.

The most significant change was that golfers were not allowed to remove the flagstick because it was an opportunity for contact between golfers. Various devices were employed to eliminate having to touch the flagstick when removing your ball after a putt. Our course chose to cut a six-inch strip of pool noodle and wrap it around the stick. The flagstick was inserted into the hole, which prevented the ball from entering the cup. The rule was that if you hit the noodle with your putt, it was scored as a successful shot, even though it would bounce away.

I never realized it until later, but several premonitions occurred before the earthshattering event on May 18, 2020. The first of these happened two days before while Irene and I were golfing with Dave and Roxanne. At one point, I remember telling them that with my luck, the only time I will ever get a hole-in-one is during a time when there is a pool noodle that prevents the ball from dropping.

Two days later, two other prophetic events occurred. In the morning, I had to phone ATB because, for some reason, I was locked out of my online banking. When I told the lady that my email address was live2golfaholein1, she was confused. When I explained that it meant "Live to golf a hole in one," she told me that she understood and hoped it would happen for me someday.

Later that day, Harold and I were golfing. As we finished hole 5, he showed me where his son had hit the ball the day before. It hit one inch to the left of the hole, and you could still see the indent where the ball had struck. He commented that if it had landed in the front, they would have had to argue about whether it was a hole-in-one. And then, the following happened.

The date is May 18, 2020. Interestingly, I wrote on Facebook the day before that I would no longer be writing blogs. I had done it for 45 days in a row, and I was *done like dinner*. However, when you receive a request from an authority above your pay grade for one last encore, how can you refuse?

We have all been to concerts, where the band plays the supposed last song of the night. However, it is not the song everyone came to hear. They finish the piece and leave the stage but are just waiting for the audience to cheer and clap until they return for the "finale," where they end on a high note by playing the song that made them famous.

There were probably many people cheering that I would not be writing anymore. I have no false illusions that any of you were standing, holding your breath until I returned to the stage. Let me tell you what changed my mind, less than 12 hours after I announced I was going into writing retirement.

Many of you know that, in the past, I sometimes have exaggerated or stretched the truth just a "tiny" bit to make a point. You won't believe what I am about to tell you. It sounds like one of those "Stranger than fiction" events that make for a great movie. I don't know that I believe in karma or coincidence, but you can be the judge.

Irene and I had a tee time booked with the Angles for 1:00 pm. When it started to rain at 12:30, I phoned the clubhouse to cancel our time. A couple of hours later, the sun came out, and with the warm temperatures and no wind, the conditions were perfect. I called Harold, and the two of us decided to play nine holes without the wives.

We had our typical game, where I would hit the ball into a tree and drop down behind it. Meanwhile, Harold would go through the same tree and end up on the green. Harold would then sink a 50-foot putt while I would 3-putt from six feet away.

After seven holes, we were within one stroke of each other and playing our usual "bogey" golf. Hole eight is a par three and was playing about 170 yds long. Even though Harold had the honours, he was taking too long, and I decided to hit first. I was still upset about chunking my chip shots on the last three holes.

I pulled out my 5-wood and let the ball rip. For the first time, all day, the shot flew high and looked like it was travelling in the right direction. Harold was so surprised that he had to comment on it. He indicated that it was looking like a relatively good shot for a change. Not that Harold and I would ever give each other the gears.

I watched the ball climb high and then start to descend. From the tee box, it looked to me like it landed on the green, about six feet in front of the pin. I could see it rolling slowly forward, and just before it stopped, I noticed it veer, straight left, before stopping a couple of inches from the cup.

So therein lies my dilemma. Any other year, when you score a hole-in-one, you have to remove it from the bottom of the cup. Since my ball hit the styrofoam noodle and bounced to the side, it could not drop in the hole. So, thanks to that &%$#@ Coronavirus, there will always be some doubt about the validity of my "Ace." There will forever be an asterisk beside it, indicating that it was in some way, tainted and not a true victory. Perhaps there will be a new category of holes in one created, and we will call it a "Lowell-orona."

On the positive side, it probably saved my life. If you remember from a previous post, I had indicated that my perfect death would be dying from a quick heart attack after scoring my first hole-in-one. So, thanks to the Golf Gods and their sick sense of humour, they were able to give me what I have always wanted without me having to expire. Some of you will disagree that the hole-in-one was legitimate, but in my mind, in another 30 years, my memories will include pulling the ball out of the hole.

As my friend Harold said right after, "It's fitting that you were there when I got my hole-in-one, and I was there when you kind of got yours." It puts a whole new spin on the adage, "You show me yours, and I'll show you mine!"

Just so everyone is clear, while we do tease each other often, Harold is a very sincere person and he was genuinely excited for me when this occurred.

Lowell's Covid-19 "Hole-in-One," May 18, 2020

I Have an Uncle Named Lowell

For years, I watched golf on television and thought it would be exciting to be there, up close, observing the golfers in person. When we retired to become Snowbirds, we started spending our winters in Arizona. Since the PGA, LPGA, and Champions Tour all have events in Phoenix, the opportunity to volunteer became a reality.

People are surprised when I tell them we have to pay $60 to volunteer. In return for our payment, we receive a logoed golf shirt, hat, and jacket. As well, we usually get up to 10 passes that we can give to our friends for free entrance to the tournament. The best perk we receive is with the Ladies Founders Cup Tournament. We receive a complimentary round of golf at the exclusive Wildfire Golf Course. This course typically costs around $130 per round, so along with the clothing and free tickets, this is a great deal.

The LPGA Founders Cup occurs in March and features all the top women golfers from around the world. The current professional men golfers compete in January at the Waste Management Tournament. We have never volunteered to work at this tournament because it is pretty much a gong show. On any given day, there can be more than 100 000 spectators, and trying to marshal the crowds is like herding cats.

Each year, however, we go as spectators to sit on hole 16, famous for being the largest accumulation of drunks in any single sporting event. It is a par three, and crowds completely encircle the hole from tee to green. It doesn't matter whether it is Tiger Woods or Rory McIllroy. If the player does not land the ball on the green, the entire gallery boos their efforts.

I have no idea how this tradition of booing began as golf generally is known for its etiquette of silence and respectful applause. Many golfers enjoy the change of pace, and some of them get the crowd going even before they hit the ball.

The first time I got involved volunteering was in 2012, at the Accenture Match Play tournament, outside of Tucson. I worked as a marshal on the fifth hole. For me, one of the most memorable moments happened during one of the practice rounds and involved a golfer from Japan by the name of Ryo Ishikawa.

When he drove his ball, he ended up slicing it wide to the right, over a fence, and into the rocks. Usually, especially during a practice round, the golfer would just tee up another ball and move on. As soon as he hit the ball, the golfer seemed very agitated. He turned to some of the spectators who followed him and started speaking excitedly in Japanese. This player ended up driving to where the ball went out of bounds and climbed over the fence to search for it. Several of the spectators went out as well to help look. They spent a good 20 minutes looking for the ball before finally giving up.

While this, in itself, was odd, it got stranger, when a half-hour later, a golf cart with his caddy and another helper drove back to where the ball went out of bounds, and they continued the search for the lost ball. I would love to know what was so "special" about that one ball and whether they ever found it.

Since that initial start as a marshal, helping out on one of the holes, I quickly realized I would prefer to walk around with the groups of golfers. There are two positions that require volunteers to walk around. The first being the standard-bearer. This position requires you to carry the big score sign to let the crowd know the current score of the golfers in your group. It is relatively easy to get on as a standard-bearer as many of the volunteers are a little older and don't want to walk the entire 18 holes.

The other position is walking scorer, where you are responsible for keeping track of the scores and relaying that information to the announcers on television. It involves a good working knowledge of the rules, and it took several years before I worked my way up to that most coveted of positions.

The best thing about walking "inside the ropes" with the players and their caddies is that we have the best seats in the house. You are often standing within feet of them while they strike their balls. You hear the players talking to their caddies about strategy, and of course, you hear the sometimes interesting things coming out of their mouths after an errant shot.

I must admit that I enjoy working with the women golfers the most. This is not only because they are so much easier to look at than a bunch of guys over 50. The biggest plus is that they appreciate all we do to help. They do not receive the same adoration as the men, and there is no parity when it comes to payouts for winning. They tend to be much less narcissistic and will visit with you as you walk along.

At the beginning of each round, the players will come up to us at the #1 tee-off box, introduce themselves and shake hands. A few years back, I worked the Founders Cup, and Jackie Stoelting, a golfer out of Florida, came up and introduced herself and shook my hand. When I told her my name, she asked me to repeat it and spell it. When I did, she smiled and said, "My husband has an Uncle Lowell; that is not a very common name."

A few minutes later, her caddie came up to me and introduced himself as Travis. When I told him my name, he looked surprised and proceeded to tell me he had an Uncle named Lowell. Being the genius that I am, I immediately deduced he must be married to Jackie. We ended up having a great walk, and I was lucky enough to get to know the couple as we talked about different things along the way.

It is customary for the golfers to give the standard-bearer and walking scorer autographed golf balls at the end of the round. When I received the ball from Jackie, I was surprised to see that not only had she signed it but also addressed it, "To Uncle Lowell." If you talk about meaningful possessions that we acquire over our lives, this one is right up there for me.

Golf ball autographed by Jackie Stoelting, 2017

My Doppelganger

It has been several years since I discovered I might have a look-alike who is somewhat of a celebrity. Of course, when it first came to my attention, I immediately thought of George Clooney or perhaps Tom Cruise or maybe even Brad Pitt. To my utter shock and amazement, it was none of those three.

The first person to suggest that I resembled someone else was a golfer from Medicine Hat, who came out once a week to enjoy the Bow Island Golf Course. I was running the pro shop, and the first time we met, he called me Jerry. I politely told him my name was Lowell, and it was nice to meet him. He explained that I had an uncanny resemblance to a professional golfer by the name of Jerry Kelly.

I had no idea who this Jerry was, so I didn't think anything of it. It wasn't until the winter, down in Arizona, that I was reminded of my "twin." We had become friends with snowbirds from all over Canada and the US. Several people from Wisconsin began to call me Jerry as well. Mr. Kelly is from Wisconsin and was a favourite golfer of theirs.

Even up to the present, it seems more and more people will stop me in places, such as Sport Chek, and ask me if I know that I look like ... and before they can tell me, I say Jerry Kelly. Although Jerry is 13 years younger than me, I was starting to believe that maybe there was some resemblance.

I have worked at the Charles Schwab Senior Golf tournament since 2015. I started as a standard-bearer, and for the last three years, I have worked as a walking scorer. The golfers must be at least 50 years of age to play on the Senior Tour. Since I follow the Tour throughout the year, I was very excited when I learned that Jerry Kelly would reach the "magic number of 50" starting in 2017.

The Charles Schwab tournament is the last tournament of the year, and this is when the overall champion is crowned, based on total winnings for the year. There are only 34 players who qualify for this final tournament. To be invited to Phoenix, the golfers need to have won enough money to qualify. Since this was Jerry's first year on this tour, I was unsure how successful his inaugural year would be.

A couple of weeks before the tournament, the list of qualifiers is posted, and I was ecstatic to see that he had indeed qualified. I began to think that maybe there was a "chance" I might get to meet my look-alike. If the stars were aligned, there was a chance I could be selected to work with his group.

There are 30 walking scorers in total. With us only working three out of the five days, the odds of being paired with him were not great. We don't find out who our pairings are until an hour before we work. When I looked at the players' list and saw Jerry's name, my heart sank. I had missed being assigned to him by only two groups.

Nan, our Committee Chair, did not like moving people around because then everyone starts requesting who they would like to be with and hard feelings can result. It is much simpler and more fair to make the process completely random. I felt I just had to explain to Nan how badly I wanted to be with Jerry, but she told me she was sorry and nothing could be done about it. Everything was set.

I was disappointed, but it was not the end of the world. I usually arrive an hour early, as you never know how Phoenix traffic will be. I sat down and was having a coffee and donut with a couple of other volunteers. I was sitting where I could see our check-in table and noticed one of the scorers walk up and talk to Nan. I saw Nan point at me, and the scorer walked over to me. He explained that he needed to finish a little earlier to make a doctor's appointment. He wondered if I could switch times with him. It made no difference to me, so I said sure.

When I asked him which golfers he was with, you won't believe what he said. You are probably thinking, I am going to say, Jerry Kelly. And you would be RIGHT. The Golf Gods had smiled upon me. Not only was I in a group with Jerry, but also Scott McCarron, who was one of the top golfers on tour. The date of November 11, 2017, is indelibly etched in my brain since that was when I was finally able to meet my "Doppelganger."

At the beginning of the round, I was a little disappointed as Jerry did not come over to shake hands with us before teeing off. He seemed to be very focused on the upcoming round of golf. We played the round, and neither Jerry nor Scott had stellar rounds, so there was a somber mood throughout. It was hole 11, where one of the marshals at the tee stopped me and asked if Jerry was my brother. I have to admit that it did make me smile a little.

After the round, the two golfers and I went into the scoring tent, where they need to verify each other's final scores. I am available for help if there are any discrepancies in their scores. Once the scorecards are signed, they transform into different people. Instead of the serious, no-nonsense persona, they all of a sudden become almost "human." The way they start to joke and laugh, it is like we are all sitting together, having a beer.

It is during this time when they autograph a golf ball for us, as a thanks for helping out. When Scott McCarron gave me his ball and shook my hand, he looked at me, then at Jerry, then at me again. He started to laugh and told Jerry that he didn't know he had a brother. We all joined in laughing, and Jerry was kind enough to pose for a pic with me, for posterity's sake.

Irene does not see much of a resemblance between us, but I will leave it up to you to decide. The best part of our meeting was that I was able to tell Jerry that the next time someone came up to him and informed him that he looks like Lowell Leffler, he would now know who they were talking about.

**Lowell and Jerry Kelly at the
Charles Schwab Tournament, Nov. 11, 2017**

Elvis Lives

When we purchased our home in Florence, Arizona, we did so, sight unseen. We had never even visited Arizona before. Having watched many Hollywood westerns growing up, I envisioned Arizona as a flat desert with cactus as the only vegetation growing in the sand.

The biggest surprise during our first visit to Arizona was that there were so many mountains and hills everywhere you look. While these were not as majestic or tall as our Rocky Mountains, they are still a dominant part of the surrounding landscape. From our house, it was less than a 20-minute drive to the closest of these hills.

For the first several years that we spent our winters in Arizona, our recreation involved mainly golf. Through golf, we ended up meeting many snowbirds from across the Northern States, Saskatchewan, and Manitoba. We became very close friends with some of our Saskatchewan neighbors, such as the Langs, Fuchs, and Montgomerys.

It wasn't until Deb and Cam Lang invited us to accompany them in their 4-seater ATV that we discovered another world in the nearby mountains. We travelled trails that only off-road vehicles or hikers would visit. Little did we know at the time that the Langs had an ulterior motive for inviting us along. Their modus operandi was to invite an unsuspecting couple along with them. They knew full well that these victims would quickly become addicted to this 4-wheeling and need to purchase a vehicle of their own.

During the summer of 2015, an old friend came to the golf course in Bow Island, where I was working. While talking to Brad, I discovered that he had a four-year-old Polaris RZR 800 with only 79 miles clocked. When he indicated that he would sell it, I jumped at the opportunity, and we became the proud owners of a "Quad."

The date was Oct. 2016, and we were back in Arizona and ready to take our new RZR on its maiden voyage. Along with Cam and Deb Lang and Vern and Connie Robinson, we set out on our first adventure using our very own quad. Little did we know what was in store for us.

The first challenge we encountered was called *The Elvis Trail*. It is a rock waterfall made up of a multitude of boulders of varying sizes. The reason it is called the Elvis Trail is that when you drive it, you rock and roll. You basically have to set your tires on one side or the other and climb over each boulder. If you are not positioned correctly, you slide off the rock. The unit bangs down, and it feels like something is coming through the floorboards.

I have never really liked going up this trail, even as a passenger. Driving my "new" quad up, I hated it much more. When we finally reached the summit, I felt like at least the worst part was over, and now we could enjoy the ride. Wrong again.

We proceeded on to the next obstacle called *O Sh*t Hill*. If you wonder why that is the name, I can vouch that it is the term most people use all the way up. It is a very steep hill where you have to get up enough speed so that you don't spin out on the loose rocks and slide all the way down. Since the steering does not work very well when you are sliding backward, out of control, this is not something you want to experience.

At one point in the climb, one or both of the front tires leave the ground, and it seems as if you will flip over backward. The secret to getting up is to put the pedal to the metal and hope for the best. We were not well prepared for the bumpy ride up. Just before we got to the top, our cooler flipped off the back. When you get to the top, there is barely enough room to stop and turn around. Since the summit is the end of the trail, the only alternative is to go back down the way you came up. Before doing this, we had to walk down to pick up our food and drinks that were scattered beside the cooler.

Once we got down the hill, I was not a happy camper since I had never driven a quad before and felt pretty incompetent after that experience.

The next part of the trip was relatively mild compared to what we had endured previously. The *Box Canyon Trail* is a narrow, dry streambed carved through the mountain. This route was used by the early stagecoaches and pony express to travel from Tucson to Globe. It is not uncommon on this trail to see animals such as mountain sheep either climbing or perched on the mountain top.

After Box Canyon, we climbed up to Granny's Pass and then on to the Martinez Mine. This mine was very isolated and difficult to get to. When it was still active, it employed many workers who lived out there for weeks at a time. There is an area carved out of the mountain with several tiny openings, making a number of small rooms. Rumor has it that "Ladies of the Night" would spend time there, making sure to separate the lonely men from some of the hard-earned money.

That day, we ended up putting over 45 miles on our unit, and by the time we got back to the trailer and car, my mind was fried. Our guides thought they had played a hilarious trick on us and asked how we had enjoyed the day. I cannot print the exact words I spoke, but I was very emphatic that on a scale of 1 to 10, with ten being the best, this ride was a -5.

I have talked earlier about Karma, and interestingly enough, both Cam and Vern ended up getting a visit from this lady who has a very long memory. We were on another ride near Montana Mountain. Pat and Bruce Maddox were riding with the Langs when Cam came too close to a washout. In slow motion, we watched as their unit gently tipped over onto its side. No one was injured, but it was still scary to see everyone hanging by their seatbelts. The only injuries were to the paint job on their quad.

Seeing the accident, Vern turned around, and as he came down to help, he hit the same ridge and tipped his machine over as well. At that point, we decided to take our unit up a different approach and kept all our wheels on the ground. I did not wish ill harm on these guys, but I must admit I smiled a little inside, knowing that what goes around comes around.

**Irene and Lowell on the first ride
with their new Quad, Oct, 2016**

Like a Fine Wine

I never met a sport I didn't like. In school, I played all the usual sports such as volleyball, basketball, badminton, and track. Being of small stature, I could never be as fast or as aggressive as my teammates. I always had to be quicker and try harder, or I would not crack the lineup.

This inspired me to always give it everything I had, despite the ravages that it might do to my body. The one advantage I did have was agility and body control, unlike many of my larger friends who had to grow into their bodies.

Once out of school, I became very interested in distance running, golf and slowpitch. I must admit that I became somewhat adept at each of these, and they provided exercise and entertainment all through my adulthood.

There were, however, two sports that I did not take up until much later than most people. The first of these was ice hockey. Growing up in the small hamlet of Grassy Lake, the only artificial ice was in the curling rink. For those who aren't familiar with curling, it is a code name for men getting out of the house so they could stay up drinking until the early morning hours.

While we did manage to find ice for skating during cold weather, I never played hockey. My parents both worked, and there was no way to drive me to a town with organized hockey. While I did learn to skate, I had no idea how to use a hockey stick.

Everything changed when I went to university in Calgary. My friend Hal was very proficient at hockey, and he talked me into playing in a recreation league, composed mainly of players with lived in residence. It was actually more of a beer league than a recreational league, so I figured what was the worst that could happen?

I need to point out that our games were played between midnight and 7:00 in the morning, as these were the only times that we could get cheap ice. It was not uncommon for many players to come to the game directly from a party, where they had usually drunk too much. Hal's girlfriend, now wife, Penny, and Irene were the only two fans crazy enough to come out at those ungodly hours to cheer us on. How could we not marry them for such dedication?

I will never forget my first game as a hockey player. I had managed to borrow odds and ends of equipment from various friends who played. The problem was that I had no idea of the order in which the gear should be put on. I basically sat there, watching everyone else get dressed. I had worn a jockstrap for basketball, so I knew that my can had to go on first. After that, I was at a loss.

I had never seen or used a garter belt and was not even sure if guys should be wearing one. I slowly dressed, trying not to make it blatant that I had no idea what I was doing. After what seemed an eternity, I finished. I knew it was time to stop dressing when there was nothing left on the bench to put on.

I don't remember much of the game except that once in a while, someone would pass me the puck. I would look wildly around for someone to hand it to so I wouldn't have to skate with it. After the game, I was exhausted but happy, as I felt that everything went better than I could have hoped. My enthusiasm was dashed when we went to meet Irene and Penny. The two of them were laughing, and I could tell that it was about me. They quickly explained that I looked pretty spiffy out there except that my socks were put on backward. I guess if that was my biggest mistake, at least they got a little entertainment for staying up so late.

I did go on to play a lot of hockey when we moved to Enchant. It was actually very motivating for me. While everyone else complained about getting older and slower, I had not yet reached my prime and improved every game. I think I won the "most improved" player three or four years in a row. To a good hockey player, that might be kind of insulting, but for me, it showed that I was getting better.

The other sport that I started later in life was a strange game called pickleball. I had never heard of this game before spending our winters in Arizona. For those who don't know anything about pickleball, it is a cross between tennis, badminton, and ping pong. You play on a court similar to badminton. Instead of a bird, you use a plastic whiffle ball with holes in it. The rackets are solid like ping pong paddles.

Pickleball is currently the fastest-growing sport in North America. It is a game that you can play at any age. As you get older, the speed of play decreases, but you learn to play smarter. We have now imported the sport to the Bow Island area, and after less than a year, our numbers have gone from 8 to 45. I do not doubt that these numbers will continue to climb. We can utilize the skating arenas when the ice has been removed, providing an opportunity for these facilities to see full-time usage.

The ironic thing about pickleball is that in all my years of playing sports, I have never had as many injuries as I have had from this one sport. I have pulled hamstrings in both legs, torn tendons, and lost a lot of skin from rolling on the cement or asphalt. And it is not just me. I have seen countless people come out the first time and end up limping home where they have to heal for a few weeks before coming back.

I am convinced that the reason for it being such a dangerous sport is that we have long memories. I, for one, can remember how fast and agile I used to be and when it comes time to lunge for a ball, my brain says, "go for it," and my body says, "not bloody likely."

I plan on playing this game for many years to come and look forward to what exciting new game I can take up when I turn 80.

How Much Land Does a Man Need?

I believe I was in grade nine at the Chamberlain School in Grassy Lake when I read a short story by the Russian author, Count Lev Nikolayevich Tolstoy. Better known as Leo Tolstoy, he wrote a classic piece of literature in 1886. When I first read it, I would have only been about 14 years old.

I am not sure why it had such a profound effect on me at such an early age, but it comes back to me more often as I get older. It may have something to do with the line graph that life insurance sales-people show you. You know the one where the left end of the line is when you are born, and the right side depicts your demise. Now that I am much closer to the right than the left, this article's significance becomes much more pronounced. I never realized that this line is also an accurate representation of how my political leanings have changed over time.

For those who have never read Tolstoy's famous story before, I will summarize it below.

There once was a peasant named Pahom who owned no land. He often thought things would be different if only we had his own land. He vowed to spend the rest of his life doing what was necessary to acquire land. However, once he started, it seemed that there was never enough.

One day a passing land dealer had returned from the land of the Bashkirs. This land was far away, but land prices were extremely reasonable. He had bought thirteen thousand acres of land, all for only 1000 rubles; approximately $13.52 US. This was more than ten times as much land as Pahom currently owned. So Pahom left his family and started on the journey, taking his servant with him. They finally came to a place where the Bashkirs had pitched their tents.

The Bashkirs seemed very glad to see him. The chief listened for a while and told him to choose whatever piece of land he wanted. "And what will be the price?" asked Pahom. "Our price is always the same," the chief replied, "the price is one thousand rubles for as much land as you can walk around in a day."

"There is one condition: If you don't return on the same day to the spot whence you started, your money is lost." "You may make as large a circuit as you please, but before the sun sets, you must return to the place you started from. All the land you cover will be yours."

The next morning, the chief took off his fox-fur cap, placed it on the ground, and said, "This will be the starting mark. Start from here, and return here again. All the land you go round shall be yours." Pahom took out his money and put it on the cap.

Pahom started walking. After having gone a thousand yards, he stopped, dug a hole, and placed pieces of turf one on another to mark his progress. He continued on. After a while, he dug another hole and kept repeating the process. It was growing warmer, so he took off his undercoat, flung it across his shoulder, and went on again. It had grown quite warm by then. As he looked at the sun, it was time to think of breakfast.

After a short break, he started on his way again. He thought to himself that he would go on for another three miles before turning left. The further he went, the better the land seemed to get.

By the time he finally decided to turn, he was sweating profusely and was very thirsty. It was sweltering, and he began to grow tired. By noon, he knew that he had to rest awhile. He was afraid to lie down, lest he fell asleep. After sitting a little while, he went on again. He went a long way in this direction and was about to turn to the left again when he perceived a damp hollow, "It would be a pity to leave that out," he thought. "flax would do well there." He continued past the hollow and dug a hole on the other side before turning the corner.

Realizing that he had made the first two sides too long, he decided to make the third one shorter. He went along the third side, stepping faster. Seeing that the sun was getting lower in the sky, he knew that he must hurry back in a straight line. By now, he was walking with difficulty. He longed to rest, but it was impossible if he meant to get back before sunset.

He looked toward the sun. Pahom was still far from his goal, and the sun was already near the rim. He began running. He threw away his coat, his boots, his flask, and his cap and kept only the spade, which he used as a support.

Pahom went on running. Though afraid of death, he could not stop. As he drew near the end of his journey, he heard the Bashkirs yelling and shouting to him. He gathered his last strength and ran on. Pahom could see the people on the hill waving their arms to hurry him up. He could see the fox-fur cap on the ground and the money on it.

He reached the top of the hill and saw the cap. There sat the Chief laughing and holding his sides. Pahom uttered a cry when his legs gave way, and he fell forward. With his last breath, he reached the cap with his hands. "Ah, that's a fine fellow!" exclaimed the chief. "He has gained much land!"

Pahom's servant came running up and tried to raise him, but he saw that blood flowed from his mouth. Pahom was dead! The Bashkirs clicked their tongues to show their pity. His servant picked up the spade and dug a grave long enough for Pahom to lie in and buried him in it. Six feet from his head to his heels was all he needed.

Irene and I have already purchased our 6-foot plots in the Bow Island Cemetery. We will spend the rest of eternity, not far from the tee-off box on hole #9 of the golf course. Our plots are beside my parents. Our land cost us $18 484.29 rubles each. If you wish to visit us in the future, you will find us in section B, block 14, plots 9 and 10. We will continue to practice our social distancing, as we will be at least six feet below anyone who comes to visit.

I Had a Vision

I have always believed in God, Heaven, and life after death, however I never saw us as having wings and flittering from cloud to cloud, in a constant state of euphoria. Deep down, I knew that the human body and mind are complex entities that would not just "end" at the time of death. We each have an internal energy that some describe as a spirit.

Albert Einstein was the first to state that energy can neither be created nor destroyed. If that is the case, then the resultant energy expended from the body at the second of death has to go somewhere. Thanks to a dream I had the other night, I now know what happens to this energy and how it affects us. Let me describe my vision and what a typical day of the afterlife involves. It was an out-of-body experience where I was looking down and observing myself. Here is what I saw.

I get up in the morning. I have sex. I consume a nutritional breakfast before heading off to the golf course. There I have sex again. I bask in the warm sun, and after my energy levels resume, I have sex a couple of more times. Now it is time for lunch, and once again, I am very conscious of eating healthy. I make sure to consume lots of greens. It is then time for another romp around the golf course. The rest of the afternoon is pretty well taken up by sex with as many partners as I can find.

By now, I am famished, and I head home for supper. After eating, I am re-energized, and it's back to the golf course. The rest of the evening is filled with more, you guessed it, sex. Once it's dark, I return home to catch up on some much-needed sleep.

The following day, I wake up, and it starts all over again. It pretty much sounds like the life of a snowbird in the winter, doesn't it? The only catch was that I was not a snowbird. I was a rabbit on a golf course in Arizona.

Death by Blogging

I don't know how many of you have heard the exciting news that I have been contacted by the World Health Organization. They are offering me $100 000 000 for the rights to help me publish my book.

It seems that after four months of testing, they have come up with some very conclusive results. NOT one person, who has faithfully read each of my daily blogs, has ever contracted or been diagnosed with the Coronavirus. The only stumbling block is having it translated into every language so the entire world can be protected.

Wouldn't that be a great way to end my life story? Alas, the reasons are much less lucrative or exciting. I have to be honest and admit that, after four months of faithful persistence, I have been flirting with the idea of wrapping up my "little" blog project. It was starting to feel like work.

I began to feel the pressure of the deadline of having to publish by 7:00 a.m. each morning. I would be lying in bed, at night and an idea for a post would come to me. I would end up having to go to my computer to write it down, while it was still fresh in my memory banks. This pressure was all self-imposed since I was not making a lot of money doing this. By not a lot, I mean zero.

I kept thinking that each time I wrote an article, it got me a little closer to completing my book. I have no aspirations of becoming an acclaimed writer or winning a Pulitzer Prize. My goal is to write something with a little humour in it, some highlights of my past, and a few of my somewhat limited nuggets of knowledge.

This experience has provided me with the opportunity to reconnect with some people with whom I had lost touch over the years. It has also allowed me to maintain contact with all of our snowbird friends, who we otherwise have to wait until the pandemic ends, to visit.

The biggest surprise for me has been the range of my audience's ages. I assumed people around my age would relate to many of my stories. It was interesting to discover that much younger people often found a story or two that they were interested in.

While many people will not look back fondly on the pandemic of 2020, I must admit that it has been an opportunity for me to take my lemons and make some "lemonade." If I had not been forced to quarantine and stay inside, life would have continued to get in the way of my goal of writing an autobiography.

Spending a few hours each day writing down my thoughts has been very therapeutic and probably prevented insanity from overwhelming me. And most assuredly, it has been a lifesaver for Irene, as it kept me out of her hair for a little while, each day.

I cannot imagine another opportunity when I would have had the time or motivation to complete a task such as this. What started, almost as a joke or a dare, evolved into a passion where I felt it was my duty to help all my friends and family get through this difficult time. When I threatened to write a daily blog, I had no intention of carrying through with my threat. It has turned out to be one of the most fulfilling and humbling experiences of my life. I could not believe that I would have had enough things to say that would interest anyone.

I have previously retired from careers twice in my lifetime, and each time, I knew when it was time to quit. I never want to be known as the person who hung on for too long before fizzling out. I have always believed it is better to *git, while the getting is good*. I am not saying I will never again write something. However, it will only be when or if I ever have something important to say. It is a strange feeling when you "bare your soul" to people, to the extent that they know more about you than they ever wanted to.

A big thank you to each one of you for your "likes," "loves," and comments on Facebook. They were very motivating for me, and receiving feedback throughout the day, always brought a smile to my face. Please stay in touch and hopefully, when all this is a distant memory, we can get together in person and maybe even share a hug.

The End

I have been blessed with a life that was more than anyone deserves. While I never grew up surrounded by wealth, there was always an abundance of love. My parents were excellent role models for us. They believed in hard work, good friends, having enough to eat, and knowing how to enjoy themselves and have fun.

I was so fortunate to have met Irene, who was the main reason I settled down and became a productive adult. I wish I could say we raised three amazing children, but I never believed in taking credit for others' accomplishments. Irene was always there, at home with the children, while I was either working or attending conferences for far too many nights and weekends. However, I did manage to find time to teach them all to ride a bicycle and drive a car.

We could not have been blessed with three better children. Andrea, Dustin, and Courtney were generally "dream" children who seldom caused grief or regret. They were not only motivated and hard-working, but they were caring and kind. They are the "BEST."

I can remember Andrea and Dustin asking us why they never had a curfew. All their friends had specific times when they had to be home. We always told them that they could decide when it was appropriate to come home. To be honest, they were generally earlier than I would have expected.

I have always wanted to leave this world, giving back more than I took. I believe that having taught in the classroom and serving as a principal and superintendent, I have positively influenced the lives of thousands of students and hundreds of teachers. While you never become wealthy in a monetary sense as a teacher, the reward of seeing your students mature and become successful adults is priceless.

Irene and I always tried to contribute to all the communities we lived in. That involved going to church and being a part of our children's lives in school and sports.

When we lived in Enchant, I was a member of the Lion's Club, and while this was mainly a social activity, we did raise funds for various community projects. I also played slow-pitch and hockey with many of the fathers of children who attended the school where I was principal.

When we moved to Foremost, we spent hours in the ice arena, flipping burgers and making french fries. With three kids in hockey and figure skating, we were expected to volunteer, as that is what you do in a small town. As the school principal, it was essential to the community to have someone that parents and students could relate to.

While in Foremost, I also served as an ambulance driver and attendant. I did this for several years. The big downside to doing this is that in a small town that you know everyone, you are dispatched to help in an emergency. While most of the time, our calls were not of the "life-threatening" variety, it was a horrendous car accident that resulted in my not being able to continue as an ambulance attendant. One of the accident victims was a high school student I was teaching at the time. As I held her in my arms and she drew her last breath, the feeling of helplessness was something I could never overcome.

Professionally, I became an active member of our Superintendent's Association, known as CASS. I served several years in our region before working my way to the Provincial Vice-President position. The year I was to become President was when we learned of Irene's breast cancer. It was a straightforward decision for me to realize that the last thing our family needed was me spending more time away from home.

As I said, we were always regular members of our local parishes. I volunteered for several years acting on the Catholic Church Board, which was responsible for three churches in Bow Island, Foremost, and Etzikom.

Being an avid golfer, I always joined the local golf leagues. These included Enchant, Foremost, and Bow Island. While I served on the executive at Enchant and Foremost, I instead managed the Bow Island Golf Course for ten years after I retired from education.

Our most incredible legacy has been our eight amazing grand-children. Olivia, Sloane, Brody, Cohen, Maeve, Chloe, Greta, and Briar are the most precious gifts we could have ever hoped for. They bring so much joy to our lives, especially as we moved from contributing citizens to join the retired and unemployed ranks. We always enjoyed our winters in Arizona, with the only regret being that we were away from the grandchildren during that time.

After 67 years of a fascinating life and 46 years of marriage, I have no regrets. However, this does not mean I am calling it quits. I hope to have many good years ahead, and who knows, I might even experience enough unique adventures to write the sequel to my memoirs.

A Happier Ending

My timing has always been suspect and this final story is like the icing on the cake. Just a few days before this event occurred, I submitted my completed manuscript to FriesenPress for layout and publication. My Publishing Specialist, Tiffany, who has been a huge help throughout this entire process, allowed me to sneak this addition in. I think it is the perfect ending to Six Under After Five.

For several months now I have noticed that I was having trouble reading. The print seemed too small and blurry. It had been 20 years since I had LAZIK surgery to correct my vision so that I no longer needed glasses. I had a procedure that I like to call Cyclops Surgery. One eye was corrected so that I could see things at a distance. The other eye was adjusted so that it could read. Now, this may sound confusing and for the first day, it was. However, once my brain adjusted, it became absolutely normal. My vision that is. My brain will never be normal.

When I went in for a vision check, a month ago, I was informed that I had a cataract in the eye that I read with. This was not a huge surprise as I have been told for several years that I had pre-cataracts forming. Apparently, the process had sped up recently and I now needed surgery to suck out the "bad" lens and replace it with a new one.

I went in last Friday, Mar. 19, 2021 and 10 minutes later, I had a new lens inserted. Within minutes I could read better than I have for a few years. The only downside was that I could not do anything strenuous or bend at the waist for 1 week. Apparently, the pressure resulting from these activities could cause the new lens to pop out.

So, when the Angles phoned me yesterday to go golfing, I had to make a decision. It was only 5 days since my surgery. If you include the day of surgery as one of the days and the fact that we are now on daylight saving time, I calculated that I should be fine. I promised myself that I would not swing too hard and would bend at the knees to tee my ball up. I never had to worry about reaching into the hole after a putt because I never actually sink any putts.

Yesterday was supposed to be 11 Celsius and mild. However, with a strong Northwest wind blowing, that brought in snow, last night, it was COLD. I went to the golf course thinking that even if we couldn't golf, maybe we could have a couple of beers, and talk about what might have been. When the Angles suggested that they still wanted to golf, I reluctantly agreed and pulled out another jacket from my golf bag. Along with my mitts and toque, I was now ready to brave the elements.

I golfed the first hole by myself because Gloria and Harold live close to the second tee and they joined me there. Once we got into the middle of the course and the wind was blocked by the trees, the temperature was bearable. We were all playing our usual game with Gloria hitting everything straight and long down the middle. Harold and I tended to spray our shots so that we never damaged any of the grass on the fairway with our second shot. The only difference was that Harold would recover with a seeing-eye shot and then can a 50-foot putt from anywhere on the green for par. I was happy with my double and triple bogeys.

As a group, we were moving along at a great pace and it was less than an hour by the time we arrived at the 5th hole. This hole is a par 3 that was playing 140 yards. It was into the wind so I calculated that I would need a little more club to get it there. I was the last to hit after both Harold and Gloria had already teed off. When I struck the ball, Gloria announced that it looked like a pretty good shot. She didn't say finally, but I knew that was implied. Harold shouted out, "Go in the hole."

Now I wish I could say that we saw the ball fly straight toward the green, land gently in front of the pin, and then roll forward and fall into the hole. But I can't. For some reason, we started talking about something else and no one bothered to watch the shot land. I think this may be called a "senior moment." I do have an excuse for myself. Because of my surgery, I had to wear my very dark "Ray Charles" sunglasses so with the gray sky, I could not see more than 50 yards in front of me.

All the way up to the green, I kept looking for my ball and was disappointed to see that there was not a ball to be found sitting any-where on the grass surface. Thinking I must have hit over the green, I drove around to the back and was eager to see how far I was going to have to chip to get back on. As I searched, I began to think that maybe a bird had flown over and took the big egg back to its nest.

Harold finally suggested that he would go look in the hole to see if the ball was resting there. I continued looking behind the green and then I heard Harold say, "It's in the hole." I immediately dis-missed this and assumed it was him trying to pull one over on me. A couple of years before, when Harold got his hole-in-one, he was busy looking for the ball behind the green. When I informed him that his ball was in the hole, he was convinced that I had put it there myself.

When Harold told me to watch, he raised the lift on the flag, and sure enough, a ball appeared out of the hole. When we confirmed that it was a Srixon, which is what I was using, I finally believed that I had indeed scored another Ace. From a story earlier in this book, you read that I was involved in what I called a Corona-hole-in-one. This was during the beginning of the pandemic when golf courses were figuring out how to prevent players from touching the hole to get their balls out after putting.

Our course had put Styrofoam blocks in the hole, which prevented the ball from dropping. If the ball hit the foam, it was counted as a successful stroke. Of course, I hit a drive on the 8th hole that I watched roll slowly to the hole and then bounce a couple inches away after striking the foam. I was frustrated that it appeared that the only hole-in-one I would ever get would be tainted by the fact that it did not drop into the bottom of the cup. Now I can say that I am one of the few people who has ever accomplished the two different holes-in-one that Covid made possible.

I must apologize to all my friends on Facebook. Last week, I complained that after my first three rounds of golf for this year, I was frustrated and searching for the happy medium in-between pars and triple bogeys. While I am still struggling for consistency, I promise after this hole-in-one, that I will no longer complain about my golf game. At least, not for another week.

Acknowledgments

I want to thank my wife Irene for putting up with me for the last 46+ years. As I mentioned earlier in the book, the primary advantage of putting up with me for so long is that it guarantees her a place in heaven. Only a saint could have that kind of patience without committing murder. She has been my moral compass and reason for being. She was my biggest supporter and fan in the writing of this book. While I could easily get carried away and possibly cross the line, she would always help me find my way back.

I am also forever indebted to my daughter-in-law, Sarah Leffler. She is a teacher and a master of the English language. Through her editing, this book slowly evolved into the "masterpiece," at least in my eyes, that you hold in front of you. Not only did she catch any grammatical errors, but she also served as my political correctness guru. I never realized how many things that we said or thought 50 years ago that are not entirely appropriate today.

It was beneficial having the wisdom of a younger generation. I was confident that this book would appeal to those who grew up in the 50s and 60s. Through Sarah's suggestions, the book evolved into an intergenerational chronicle that will appeal to readers of all ages.

I also want to thank Dana Couillard, a friend and independent publisher of two books of his own. He co-authored the book *Lifeworth* with his brother Hal and has since published *The Three-Legged Stool*. As a new author, I had so many questions and didn't even know what I didn't know. Dana gave me the courage to challenge "The Imposter Syndrome," where we convince ourselves we are not "good" enough to be a writer. When I doubted my abilities, he reminded me to think like a navy seal. When they are faced with a dangerous situation, they simply ask, "What is the worst that can happen if I do this?"

Dana was invaluable in recommending FriesenPress publishing services, who guided me through the unknown waters of what is involved in a book coming to fruition.

Lastly, I want to thank all of my friends and family who faithfully read my blogs daily and provided me with the feedback to keep on writing. Your support continued as you helped me with designing my covers and ensuring that I never became too self-deprecating. Nonetheless, that doesn't mean you get a free book. You will need to pay just like everyone else. Remember, I am a senior on a fixed income.

About the Author

Lowell Leffler was a child of the 50s and 60s growing up in a small town. He spent his entire adult life in education as a teacher, principal, and superintendent. Lowell has always had a wild side with a need for adrenaline and the belief that he should try anything—at least once. These days, he is an avid golfer and pickleball player. In the past, he has run two full marathons. Even at the age of 67, he still runs 8 kilometers a day and rides his elliptical for an hour.

In the summer, Lowell and his wife, Irene, live in the small, southern Alberta town of Bow Island. When the temperature starts to drop, their Snowbird wings unfurl, and they spend the winter in Florence, Arizona. Together, their most significant accomplishments are their three exceptional children and eight phenomenal grandchildren.

His greatest wish is that we never lose the ability to love, laugh, and have fun. Life is too short, and none of us will get out of this alive. Don't waste a single day or even moment and never take our freedom and many blessings for granted. Each of us is one of God's masterpieces, and there will never be another you. The world is a better place because you are in it.

Lightning Source UK Ltd.
Milton Keynes UK
UKHW011844230621
386053UK00006B/331/J